"Dietrich Bonhoeffer wrote of the importance of 'worldly' preaching that speaks God's truth into the contemporary context. This excellent book will make preachers aware of the many worlds that shape the sermon. From the world of the text to the world of the preacher to the multiform world of cultural diversity, today's sermon enters a landscape that is more like a universe than a single world. Skillfully written by some of the best minds and voices in homiletics, this book will stretch your thinking and improve your preaching. I am happy to recommend it."

—**John Koessler**, author of *Folly, Grace, and Power: The Mysterious Act of Preaching*

"I first 'met' Haddon Robinson in Bible college when I read his seminal text on preaching. Through his book *Biblical Preaching*, he discipled me in preaching, impressing upon me the need to be simple, not shallow, and to connect Sunday to Monday. What Yoda was to Luke Skywalker and a generation of Jedi, Haddon Robinson is to today's preacher. While the Skywalkers of the pulpit receive inordinate praise, I'm grateful to my friend Scott Gibson for calling attention to this great Yoda of preaching and preachers."

—**Bryan Loritts**, senior pastor, Abundant Life Christian Fellowship; author of *Saving the Saved*

# The Worlds

## *of the*

# Preacher

### NAVIGATING BIBLICAL, CULTURAL, AND PERSONAL CONTEXTS

FOREWORD BY BRYAN CHAPELL

EDITED BY

## SCOTT M. GIBSON

**B**
**Baker Academic**
*a division of Baker Publishing Group*
Grand Rapids, Michigan

Published by Baker Academic
a division of Baker Publishing Group
PO Box 6287, Grand Rapids, MI 49516-6287
www.bakeracademic.com

Printed in the United States of America

ISBN: 978-0-8010-9961-8

Library of Congress Cataloging-in-Publication Control Number: 2017051451

Sections of chapter 5 have been employed and adapted from Matthew Kim, "A Blindspot in Homiletics: Preaching That Exegetes Ethnicity," *Journal of the Evangelical Homiletics Society* 11, no. 1 (March 2011): 66–83. Used by permission. Chapter 5 also incorporates some select ideas from Matthew Kim, *Preaching with Cultural Intelligence: Understanding the People Who Hear Our Sermons* (Grand Rapids: Baker Academic, 2017), particularly from chap. 6, which is on preaching and ethnicity.

18  19  20  21  22  23  24      7  6  5  4  3  2  1

In honor of
Haddon W. Robinson
1931–2017

# Contents

# Foreword

BRYAN CHAPELL

I was the "up and comer." Haddon was the reigning master. We were invited by a publisher we shared to a college campus for a joint project that would combine our instruction in one of the first-ever digital educational programs designed to teach preaching remotely.

Prior to that project I had never met Haddon Robinson. I had read, quoted, and admired this respected seminary president, homiletics professor, and author of *Biblical Preaching* (probably the most widely distributed homiletics textbook in history), but I had not enjoyed his company. I wasn't sure what to expect. His writings were filled with wisdom but presented with remarkable clarity—almost deceptively simple without being simplistic, plain yet able to inspire with poignancy. So I was not sure which Haddon Robinson I would meet: the plain preacher or the sage professor. I met both.

The technology experts took care of putting our homiletical ideas and teaching methods into digital formats, audio recordings, computer figures, and animated vignettes. Our books were sliced, diced, and enfolded into a single, comprehensive preaching course that looks primitive today (kind of like an early *Pong* video game), but it was cutting edge at the time. There simply was not enough memory capacity in most personal computers to run anything more sophisticated, and we were pioneering with theology software that now seems about as advanced as *The Lucy Show* when compared to the latest *Star Wars* film.

The one concession our engineers were able to make for designing a "human" touch into the software was allowing Haddon and me to make a brief video statement of the emphases and priorities of our books. By this time, I had been teaching preaching for several years, but my main book on preaching had only recently been published. Haddon was far more experienced as a preacher and academic, and his book was being used worldwide, establishing him as the premier teacher of preaching for that time.

I wondered how anything I would say could hold a candle to whatever he was going to say in our short video clips. So I focused hard on memorizing the preface to my book, trying to look intelligent and sound important as I recited into a TV camera the formal purposes of expository preaching with academic precision and doctoral tones. "Not bad," I thought, when I had finished. "At least I won't come across as dumb."

But then it was Haddon's turn. I don't remember the exact words that he said, but I remember how he said them. He looked at the camera, smiled, and spoke as though he were addressing a friend across the kitchen table. There was no pretense, no professorial puffery, no high-sounding oratory. He did not say "God" with three syllables and did not worry about presenting his ideas with perfection. He was quite simply as natural, caring, and human as any teacher I have ever seen in expressing his love for God's Word, his regard for the calling of preaching, and his care for the preachers we were preparing to instruct for a lifetime of proclamation.

When he was done, I confess that my first thought was, "I wish I had done that." Because of that moment and Haddon's example, I learned that I could do exactly that in the many future occasions I would have to further the work of homiletics in which we co-labored. The example of a senior statesman in my field who was so confident of the power of the Word and the strength of his thought that he could afford to be straightforward and caring in expression stuck with me. I am forever grateful to Haddon for that understanding of what it means to be a man of God as well as a professor of preaching.

Though I had been a teacher of preachers for years, I learned the reality of ethos from Haddon that day in a way that I had not previously grasped. We communicate more when we speak with plain truth and compassion for others than we do when we speak with ornateness and concern for our reputations. That's why the apostle Paul would write, "Seeing then that we have such hope, we use great plainness of speech" (2 Cor. 3:12 KJV), an expression of both boldness and clarity, echoing the ancient biblical ethic of presenting the Word of God "clearly" so that God's people can understand and act upon it (Neh. 8:8).

All these truths I knew in my head, but Haddon's writing, preaching, and visible example now made such truths more real. I realized more than ever that it is better to be understood than worshiped. Communicating the significance of God's Word is far more important than communicating our significance. The grace that has bought us and holds us is more than sufficient to establish our standing before the Lord, so that we can always afford to put the priorities of God's Word and the needs of his people above concerns to establish our own regard.

I am grateful for far more from Haddon Robinson than that single example of godly testimony and character. He was the most influential teacher of preachers for a generation, and to a good end, because he valued the proclamation of the Word above himself and valued the understanding of God's people above the badges of his own reputation. I am thankful for this book that honors his work and his legacy because I know they have been built not merely on a flair for public ministry but on a commitment to God's Word and loving people that Haddon lived daily and personally.

# Acknowledgments

There are many who help make a book like this. Thank you, contributors, for your diligent work and for your influence in the field of homiletics. We all stand with gratitude on the shoulders of Haddon Robinson.

Thank you, Bryan Chapell, for writing the foreword. Your words are insightful and true. We all owe a debt to Haddon for his incredible legacy.

Thank you, Dianne Newhall, who served Haddon Robinson as his faithful administrative assistant and who years ago transcribed "The Worlds of the Preacher" lecture that Robinson delivered at Gordon-Conwell Theological Seminary during a summer conference. Lady Di, I continue to be grateful for your willing help—which even surpasses your tenure at the seminary. Grateful for you!

Many thanks to Torrey Robinson and Vicki Hitzges, Haddon's son and daughter, who granted permission to use "The Worlds of the Preacher" lecture as the opening chapter of this book. Your generosity and foresight allow many more preachers to learn from your father's contribution to preaching, which will enrich their own preaching as well.

One could not write with appreciation about Haddon Robinson without acknowledging the immense contribution to Haddon's life made by his wife, Bonnie. Bonnie Robinson is a gem who added luster to the ministry given by God to Haddon. They shared this ministry with grace. Thank you, Bonnie!

Robert Hosack and the team at Baker Publishing Group are an incredible bunch. Thank you for your commitment to preaching and to the publication of books that further the field. Thank you for your guidance and help in the production of this book. You are appreciated more than you know.

Finally, I thank Rhonda, my wife. She is a solid, steady anchor in my many worlds. Her love is immovable and her support unwavering. Her astute edits to my contributions in this volume enrich what I wrote because of her careful eye. More than this, her love and commitment to Christ are demonstrated in beautiful markers of maturity in her life. She shows me every day what it means to live as a mature disciple of Christ. Thank you, Rhonda. I love you and thank God for you.

# Introduction

## A Tribute to Haddon Robinson

### SCOTT M. GIBSON

This book recognizes the profound contribution Haddon Robinson has made to the field of homiletics. Over his many years of teaching preaching, Robinson delivered his notable lecture "The Worlds of the Preacher." In this lecture, master of divinity and doctor of ministry students listened to Robinson encourage them to gain a 360-degree view of the worlds in which they preach. The lecture did not stay in the seminary classroom. Robinson delivered it at preaching conferences, distinguished lectureships, and Bible conferences.

When Haddon Robinson stepped up to preach, he came with his Bible in his hand and his sermon in his heart. He shared the text and he shared himself. Even though we did not see any paper notes, he had and will continue to have a noted effect in the field of homiletics. This introduction would be remiss if it did not include a sketch of Robinson's life, along with his contributions and commitments to preaching.

### Beginnings

Haddon William Robinson was born on March 21, 1931, to William Andrew and Anna Robinson, immigrants from Ireland. They made their home in the

Mousetown district of Harlem, described by *Reader's Digest* as one of the most dangerous areas in the United States.[1]

Haddon's mother died when he was ten. He became what we now refer to as a "latchkey child," raised by his father. His father was a dedicated Christian who worked during the afternoons and evenings. Haddon's grandfather had come to faith as an adult. While staggering home drunk one night, he passed a church and heard them singing:

> There is life for a look at the crucified one.
> There is life at this moment for thee.
> Look, sinner, look unto him and be saved,
> Unto him who died on the tree.
> Look, look, look and live
> To him who died on the tree.[2]

When he heard those words, Haddon's grandfather was converted and gave his life to Christ, and later became a lay preacher. Haddon's son, Torrey, comments to his sons in the dedication of the book that he and his father wrote together, *It's All in How You Tell It*:

> By God's grace, that story, that faith was passed on to your great-grandfather, to your grandfather, and then to your father. Now that story has become your story.
>
> It is our prayer that your children and your grandchildren may know the truth of that story as they see it lived out in you.[3]

Yet the truth of the gospel came to Haddon not all that gently. The rough neighborhood in which the Robinsons lived had its influence on the young boy. He associated with a gang. One night his gang was gathered for a rumble. Somehow, the police were tipped off and arrived on the scene.

A policeman approached the group in which Robinson was a member. He searched the boy and found that he had an ice pick tucked away in his clothing. "What do you plan to do with this?" barked the officer. "Chop ice," said Robinson. The officer pushed him and sent him sprawling. That night

---

1. Bradford Chambers, "Boy Gangs of Mousetown," *Reader's Digest* 53 (August 1948): 144–58. A shortened version of Haddon Robinson's biography is found in my introduction to *Making a Difference in Preaching: Haddon Robinson on Biblical Preaching*, ed. Scott M. Gibson (Grand Rapids: Baker, 1999), 11–15.

2. "There Is Life for a Look at the Crucified One," a hymn written by Amelia M. Hull.

3. Haddon W. Robinson and Torrey W. Robinson, *It's All in How You Tell It: Preaching First-Person Expository Messages* (Grand Rapids: Baker Books, 2003), 3.

changed young Haddon Robinson's life. He left the gang, which was no doubt an answer to his father's prayers.

During this time he came into contact with John Mygatt, a Sunday school teacher at the Broadway Presbyterian Church in New York City. Robinson went there to play basketball, but he got a lot more than a few good shots. Mygatt made the Bible lessons exciting.

John Mygatt loved his class of boys. He was one of the few people from the church who came to the Robinson home to visit. The Sunday school teacher made a lifelong impression on the boy from Mousetown.

Sometime during his early teens Haddon Robinson prayed the sinner's prayer and gave his life to Christ. An exceptionally bright young man, he left for college at Bob Jones University at age sixteen. While in college he became interested in preaching, spending Friday evenings in the library reading books of sermons and books about preaching. At graduation, he received the top award given to a senior for preaching. He delivered a sermon on John 3:16.

In 1951, following college, he went to study at Dallas Theological Seminary and married his college sweetheart, Bonnie Vick.

During his final year at Dallas Seminary, Robinson taught informal classes in preaching since the seminary did not offer courses in homiletics. He left Dallas in 1955 for the First Baptist Church of Medford, Oregon, where he was assistant pastor. Robinson planned to be an evangelist, but after only a few years in Oregon, the leadership at Dallas Seminary asked him to come back to teach preaching at the school. He spent nineteen years at Dallas. While there, Robinson completed a master of arts degree at Southern Methodist University in 1960 and a doctorate of philosophy in speech communication at the University of Illinois in 1964.

In 1979 he became president of Denver Theological Seminary, and in 1980 he published his celebrated textbook on preaching, *Biblical Preaching: The Development and Delivery of Expository Messages*, now in its third edition. Over 250 Bible colleges and seminaries use the book. The first edition sold more than 150,000 copies.[4]

After twelve years at Denver Seminary, Robinson was invited by Gordon-Conwell Theological Seminary to become the Harold John Ockenga Distinguished Professor of Preaching. He held the position from 1991 to 2012. Additionally, he served as president of Gordon-Conwell from 2007 to 2008.

Over those years he taught hundreds of neophyte preachers in the master of divinity program. In addition, he mentored scores of seasoned preachers in the doctor of ministry program. He wrote articles on preaching and

---

4. Karen Steele of Baker Publishing Group, email to Scott M. Gibson, October 19, 2004.

continued an active preaching schedule. In 1996, a major study conducted by Baylor University listed Haddon Robinson as one of the twelve most effective preachers in the English-speaking world.[5]

As a teenager Haddon Robinson scribbled the following in his diary about the preacher Harry Ironside: "He preached for an hour and it seemed like twenty minutes; others preach for twenty minutes and it seems like an hour. I wonder what the difference is?" Robinson spent the rest of his life trying to answer this question. We see it in his web of influence as a redeemed person in his passion for preaching, his teaching of preaching, and his publications about preaching.

## Biblical Preaching

Robinson's book *Biblical Preaching* was welcomed in 1980 with enthusiasm. One reviewer stated:

> Robinson has made a very helpful contribution to the teaching of the art of expository preaching. . . . A serious reading of this discussion and practical testing of its counsels should enhance the ability of the exegetically qualified and theologically informed preacher to expound Scripture to God's glory, the salvation of sinners and the edification of Christ's church.[6]

Another reviewer, aware of Robinson's insights and the significance of his contribution to homiletics, wrote:

> When you read this book you will want to have pen and pencil in hand so that you can mark the many "I wish I had said that" kind of statements it contains. You will also want to mark portions to which you will want to return later for further reflection.[7]

The reviewer continues:

> Beginning with the establishment of the identity of expository preaching and showing that, while most conservative preachers give assent to it, in reality they do not practice it, Robinson walks the preacher through the steps necessary to prepare sermons that truly are expositional/expository. Probably the unique

5. "Baylor Names the 12 Most Effective Preachers," Baylor University, February 28, 1996, https://www.baylor.edu/mediacommunications/news.php?action=story&story=1036.

6. Carl G. Kromminga, review of *Biblical Preaching: The Development and Delivery of Expository Messages*, by Haddon W. Robinson, *Calvin Theological Journal* 16, no. 2 (November 1981): 288.

7. Paul R. Fink, review of *Biblical Preaching: The Development and Delivery of Expository Messages*, by Haddon W. Robinson, *Grace Theological Journal* 3, no. 1 (Spring 1982): 149–50.

contribution that Robinson makes to the process is the concept of stating the sermon "idea" in subject and predicate form. While this is not new to the field of rhetoric (it can be traced back to Aristotle), few homileticians have related the concept to sermon preparation.[8]

In *Biblical Preaching*, Robinson wrote:

Those in the pulpit face the pressing temptation to deliver some message other than that of the Scriptures—a political system (either right-wing or left-wing), a theory of economics, a new religious philosophy, old religious slogans, or a trend in psychology. Ministers can proclaim anything in a stained-glass voice at 11:30 on Sunday morning following the singing of hymns. Yet when they fail to preach the Scriptures, they abandon their authority. No longer do they confront their hearers with a word from God. That is why most modern preaching evokes little more than a wide yawn. God is not in it.[9]

He continues later, "First, and above all, the thought of the biblical writer determines the substance of an expository sermon."[10] He considers the process of exposition to be that of a philosophy rather than a method. He comments: "Whether we can be called expositors starts with our purpose and with our honest answer to the question: 'Do you, as a preacher, endeavor to bend your thought to the Scriptures, or do you use the Scriptures to support your thought?'"[11] "Ultimately," writes Robinson, "the authority behind expository preaching resides not in the preacher but in the biblical text."[12]

Fifteen years later Harold Bryson acknowledged Haddon Robinson's basic philosophical commitment to the Bible and to preaching what the Bible says. He observes:

Haddon Robinson, writing in 1980, proposed a substantive idea for expository preaching. Robinson said expository preaching was "the communication of a

8. Fink, review of *Biblical Preaching*, 150.
9. Haddon W. Robinson, *Biblical Preaching: The Development and Delivery of Expository Messages*, 3rd ed. (Grand Rapids: Baker Academic, 2014), 18. Regarding gender-specific language, Robinson reflects in the second edition, "I've also changed my language to reflect my theology. God doesn't distribute his gifts by gender. Both women and men have the ability and responsibility to communicate God's Word. I have always believed that, but the language in my first book reflected a distinct male bias. To those women who have used my book in spite of that, I express my thanks for their grace. In this revision I hope I have demonstrated the fruits of my repentance." *Biblical Preaching: The Development and Delivery of Expository Messages*, 2nd ed. (Grand Rapids: Baker Academic, 2001), 10.
10. Robinson, *Biblical Preaching*, 3rd ed., 5.
11. Robinson, *Biblical Preaching*, 3rd ed., 5.
12. Robinson, *Biblical Preaching*, 3rd ed., 7.

biblical concept, derived from and transmitted through a historical, grammatical, and literary study of a passage in its context, which the Holy Spirit first applies to the personality and experience of the preacher, then through him to his hearers." According to this definition, expository preaching was more a philosophy than a method. The expositor's paramount concern was for the message of the text and how to communicate that message.[13]

Michael Quicke likewise affirmed Robinson's premise. Quicke wrote, "Robinson correctly states that expository preaching 'at its core is more a philosophy than a method.'"[14]

However, Robinson acknowledges that a step-by-step process is necessary—that is why he wrote his book. Notice the title of the book. It is called *Biblical Preaching: The Development and Delivery of Expository Messages*. By following a stage-to-stage approach, Robinson guides the preacher in the application of the philosophy. Robinson offers a clear process for sermon development. He acknowledges that such an approach is necessary—and may be surprising—to the preacher. He observes:

> My Aunt Ginny was one of the great cooks of the twentieth century. That wasn't solely my verdict. All the members of our extended family share that opinion. On Thanksgiving or Christmas we would all assemble at Aunt Ginny's house to enjoy a world-class dinner, arguably the finest feast served in New York City that day. The turkey, the stuffing, the potatoes, the gravy were all superb, but the crowning moment of the meal came when Aunt Ginny served her desserts. If there is a Platonic ideal of mince or pumpkin pie, Aunt Ginny's came as close to it as any chef on earth.
>
> You cannot imagine how stunned I was, therefore, to learn that my Aunt Ginny used cookbooks. In fact, she confessed that she got her piecrust recipe from Betty Crocker. And, furthermore, she didn't seem repentant! I thought that no world-class cook would ever take advice from someone else. Why would she follow a formula concocted by Mrs. Crocker when she could follow her own instincts for making desserts? But my Aunt Ginny was a modest woman. She knew she didn't know everything there was to know about cooking, and other devotees of the stove and oven could help her to excel.
>
> Ministers can learn a lot from my Aunt Ginny. No matter how long we've been crafting sermons, none of us has achieved perfection. All of us can still learn from others. A preacher or a teacher would do well to read at least one

13. Harold T. Bryson, *Expository Preaching: The Art of Preaching through a Book of the Bible* (Nashville: Broadman & Holman, 1995), 25.

14. Michael J. Quicke, *360-Degree Preaching: Hearing, Speaking, and Living the Word* (Grand Rapids: Baker Academic, 2003), 28.

book on preaching every year. To coin a commercial phrase, we need to think about preaching again for the first time.[15]

At this writing, *Biblical Preaching* is in its third edition, continuing to establish its place in the teaching of preaching. Haddon Robinson's contribution to the field of homiletics is invaluable. But Robinson's commitment had an end in mind: connecting the Bible to listeners.

## Connecting the Bible to Listeners

Haddon Robinson encouraged preachers to link Sunday morning's world with Monday morning's world. Sermons are to be applied to their listeners. He comments, "We should forget about speaking to the ages, therefore, and speak to our day. Expository preachers confront people about themselves from the Bible instead of lecturing to them about the Bible's history or archaeology." He continues, "Effective application thrusts [an expositor] into both theology and ethics."[16] Robinson acknowledged that connecting the dots to application is not always easy. He reflects on one of his sermons:

> It was a disastrous sermon. A church in Dallas invited me to preach on John 14. That's not an easy passage. It is filled with exegetical questions about death and the Second Coming. How do you explain, "If I go and prepare a place for you, I will come again, and receive you unto myself"? How is Jesus preparing that place? Does Jesus mean we won't go to be with him until he comes back? What about soul sleep? I spent most of my week studying the text and reading commentaries to answer questions like these.
>
> When I got up to preach, I knew I had done my homework. Though the issues were tough, I had worked through them and was confident I was ready to deliver solid biblical teaching on the assigned passage.
>
> Five minutes into the sermon, though, I knew I was in trouble. The people weren't with me. At the ten-minute mark, people were falling asleep. One man sitting near the front began to snore. Worse, he didn't disturb anyone! No one was listening.
>
> Even today, whenever I talk about that morning, I still get an awful feeling in the pit of my stomach.
>
> What went wrong? The problem was that I spent the whole sermon wrestling with the tough theological issues, issues that intrigued me. Everything I said

15. Haddon W. Robinson, foreword to *Preaching with Relevance: Without Dumbing Down*, by Keith Willhite (Grand Rapids: Kregel, 2001), 12.
16. Robinson, *Biblical Preaching*, 3rd ed., 10, 11.

was valid. It might have been strong stuff in a seminary classroom. But in that church, in that pulpit, it was a disaster.

What happened? I didn't speak to the life questions of my audience. I answered my questions, not theirs.[17]

Being aware of one's listeners was an important consideration for Haddon Robinson. Not only did he believe that the preacher is to be biblically driven, but he also wanted the sermon to be listener focused. This commitment to application and relevance is a principle that drove Robinson for decades. He wanted the sermon to make a difference in the lives of his listeners.

To remind him of his listeners, Robinson kept for decades this bit of doggerel on a plaque on his desk:

> As Tommy Snooks and Bessie Brooks
> Were leaving church one Sunday,
> Said Tommy Snooks to Bessie Brooks:
> "Tomorrow will be Monday!"

For Robinson, the Bible did not stay in the long ago and far away. The preacher must show listeners how the truth of the text makes sense today. He asserts, "All preaching involves a 'so what?' A lecture on the archaeology of Egypt, as interesting as it might be, isn't a sermon. A sermon touches life. It demands practical application."[18] He continues: "In the final analysis, effective application does not rely on techniques. It is more a stance than a method. Life-changing preaching does not talk to people about the Bible. Instead, it talks to the people about themselves—their questions, hurts, fears, and struggles—from the Bible. When we approach the sermon with that philosophy, flint strikes steel. The flint of someone's problem strikes the steel of the Word of God, and a spark emerges that can set that person on fire for God."[19]

## The Worlds of the Preacher

This volume engages with Haddon Robinson's widely recognized lecture "The Worlds of the Preacher." Contributors represent the institutions at which Robinson served: Dallas Theological Seminary, Denver Seminary, and

---

17. Haddon W. Robinson, "Blending Bible Content and Life Application," in *Making a Difference in Preaching*, 85–86.
18. Robinson, "Blending Bible Content and Life Application," 88.
19. Robinson, "Blending Bible Content and Life Application," 94.

Gordon-Conwell Theological Seminary. Writing from their areas of expertise, the authors explore aspects of the worlds that Robinson presents.

Chapter 1 is Robinson's lecture, "The Worlds of the Preacher." The lecture was presented orally and has been transcribed and edited for publication. Here, Robinson lays out the four worlds of the preacher: the ancient world of the Bible, the modern world, the world of the preacher's listeners, and the preacher's personal world.

Chapter 2 begins the book's engagement with Robinson's four worlds by considering the world of the Old Testament. Steven D. Mathewson, a former student of Robinson's and author of *The Art of Preaching Old Testament Narrative*, examines four aspects of the Old Testament world that preachers must understand when they enter it to preach to their listeners.

Chapter 3 is authored by Robinson's former Dallas Theological Seminary colleague Duane Litfin. Writing as a New Testament scholar and homiletician, Litfin focuses on a conceptual model that clarifies what preachers do: the journey from *then* to *now*.

In chapter 4, I examine the inner world of the preacher, where the preacher's character is cultivated. I provide suggestions for the preacher to foster growth and maturity in his or her life that will strengthen preaching.

Chapter 5 discusses the world of ethnic and cultural issues. Matthew D. Kim of Gordon-Conwell Theological Seminary examines three areas where a preacher may develop a robust ethnic and cultural integration in preaching.

The worlds of the listener is the focus of chapter 6. Jeffrey Arthurs of Gordon-Conwell Theological Seminary builds on Robinson's lecture by helping preachers analyze and adapt to their listeners. Specifically, Arthurs engages with stage four of Robinson's homiletic, analyzing the exegetical idea with the three developmental questions.

In chapter 7, Patricia M. Batten of Gordon-Conwell Theological Seminary opens readers' eyes to the importance of understanding the immediate context in which preachers preach. She considers elements that preachers need to know in order to be effective in their preaching within the particular churches they serve.

Victor Anderson of Dallas Theological Seminary casts a vision in chapter 8 for preaching by examining the mission of God and what that mission looks like in our present world. He challenges readers to embrace preaching that "seeks to see the image of God filling the earth."

Chapter 9 underscores the important role that history plays in our preaching. Scott Wenig of Denver Seminary encourages readers to see the value of historical insight and how an appreciation and understanding of the worlds of history will help in the exposition of Scripture.

In chapter 10, Donald R. Sunukjian, who taught with Robinson at Dallas Theological Seminary, helps preachers consider the challenge of preaching in an age saturated with images. Sunukjian skillfully demonstrates how sermons can faithfully depict the truth of the biblical text.

An afterword completes the book. More than a book that honors Haddon Robinson, the chapters in this volume are meant to advance the field of preaching by building on Robinson's homiletics.

## Conclusion

Haddon Robinson confessed, "I have come closer to being bored out of the Christian faith than being reasoned out if it. . . . I think we underestimate the deadly gas of boredom. It is not only the death of communication, but the death of life and hope."[20] His influence on and commitment to biblical preaching and to listeners has helped preachers to remain fresh and encouraged in their preaching. God made a difference in Haddon Robinson's life, and God has used Haddon Robinson to make a difference in the lives of others.

In the foreword to *Making a Difference in Preaching*, the late Keith Willhite wrote:

> Haddon Robinson himself is a preacher of difference. Anyone who has had the joy of listening to him preach has listened to interpretive insights, masterful images, and similes and illustrations that sharpen the point or the big idea with amazing precision.
>
> Years ago, a seminary classmate remarked, "I think God made Haddon Robinson and then he made the rest of us—two runs of production." I responded, "I think he made Haddon Robinson, then a bunch of other preachers, and then the rest of us. We were two runs removed." My classmate agreed.[21]

This book is dedicated to Haddon Robinson, who died on July 22, 2017, during the production of this project. Haddon Robinson understood well the worlds in which a preacher lives.

---

20. Quoted in David W. Henderson, *Culture Shift: Communicating God's Truth to Our Changing World* (Grand Rapids: Baker, 1998), 19.
21. Keith Willhite, foreword to *Making a Difference in Preaching*, 9.

# 1

## The Worlds of the Preacher

### HADDON W. ROBINSON

## Introduction

One of the surprising discoveries that archaeologists have made is that the temple in Jerusalem and the temples of pagan religions in the Near East were not radically different. Most temples that have been excavated had an outer court and an inner court that led to the holy place. The architecture of the holy place in pagan temples, like Solomon's temple, led to the holiest place of all. Everything pointed to that sacred chamber—the slant of the floors, the increasing darkness, the awe and mystery. Into that sacred chamber the pagan priest would go, sometimes once a month at the turning of the moon, or once a quarter, or even less often, only once each year. That central place was filled with mystery and awe.

In pagan religions, in the holy of holies sat a little gold idol. That god or goddess represented the sun or the moon or fertility that the people worshiped. If you look at the tabernacle and later the temple of Israel in the Bible, it too had an outer court and an inner court, it too had a holy of holies. In that holiest place of all, however, instead of a golden god, the god of war, or the goddess of fertility, was a golden box. Within that golden box were, among other things, the tablets of the law delivered to Moses on Mount Sinai.

You might think that the temple architecture was unique to the people of Israel. But what it may tell us is that what separates us from the pagans is not the shape of our buildings or even the forms of our worship. What separates men and women who take God seriously is that the center of the religion of the Bible is the revealed moral will of God. God revealed himself through history, and that revelation is contained in the Scriptures. We believe that this book is the Word of God without error, and for that reason all Christian thought must emerge from this book and all Christian preaching and teaching must be based on it.

That stands as the cardinal reason for expository preaching. If our thought must follow God's thought, then those who lead God's people must teach the Scriptures and relate the Scriptures to people's lives.

We recognize that if we are going to be teachers, we're going to be communicators. We not only have to have this supreme message, but we also want to have an understanding of the people to whom we speak. That's why some people talk about preaching being not in the shape of a circle but in the shape of an ellipse. An ellipse has two centers. We are not singly centered in the Bible, as important and crucial as that is to us; we are also centered in the men and women in the world. James Cleland calls this "bi-focal preaching."[1] It has two centers—a center in the Scriptures and a center in people today.

The central image in John Stott's book *Between Two Worlds* is that of a bridge.[2] He says that the preacher stands like a bridge between two worlds—the world of the Bible and today's world. A bridge brings two landmasses together. Two bodies of land that are separated by a river or a canyon are bridged, and the bridge brings them together. Stott argues that the expository preacher who takes the Bible and the listener seriously is like a bridge between two worlds.

Being a great communicator of God's truth, however, involves us in not just two worlds but in four worlds. One world with which we are concerned is the world of the Bible—the ancient world. It's the world we enter through exegesis, through the study of the Scriptures. It dominates us. It is crucial to our message. As preachers, we want to understand the history of the ancient world. One really cannot understand the Bible unless one understands its history.

## The First World: The Ancient World or the World of the Bible

### History

If you were to travel along the North Shore of the Boston area, you'd see a lot of little shops that sell antiques. We have one in Gloucester that

---

1. James Cleland, *Preaching to Be Understood* (Nashville: Abingdon, 1965).
2. John R. W. Stott, *Between Two Worlds: The Challenge of Preaching Today* (Grand Rapids: Eerdmans, 1980).

has on one side of the sign "We buy junk" and on the other side "We sell antiques." But let's suppose you go into one of those stores, and as you wander around you see an old trunk. Your hand springs a small lever, and there is a compartment that has obviously been hidden for a long time. You reach into that compartment and come out with a bundle of letters. They are old and faded and tied with a ribbon that once was yellow but has been touched by the years. You gingerly open them. Though the ink is dim, it is still able to be deciphered. As you read, you recognize that these are letters written by a young man to a young woman. You discover that he has apparently gone off to war. You don't have to know much else as you read those letters to get some feel for what they are about. You can understand his loneliness when he writes about it. You've felt loneliness too. You can understand his fear when he talks about comrades of his who have fallen in battle. You can understand his frustration. When he went off to fight, the motto was "Keep the eggs warm—we'll be home for breakfast." But they've grown cold. Then there are other things in those letters that you won't understand. You might have references to Bull Run, to Chattanooga. There'll be other mentions of generals and "the cause." The letters are about the Civil War. Obviously, to understand the letters, you have to understand the history.

When God chose to give us his revelation, he chose to give it to particular people at a particular place and a particular time. God spoke once to a people long ago and through those people he speaks to us. To understand the Bible, you have to know its history. If you take the Minor Prophets, for instance, and you do not understand anything about Edom, you cannot understand the book of Obadiah. If you don't understand anything about Israel and Judah, you cannot understand Hosea, and it would be more difficult to understand Amos. That is, to understand the meaning of any passage of Scripture, you must understand the history.

### Language

To understand the Bible, it's also helpful to understand the languages of the Bible—Greek and Hebrew. Let me at least file this disclaimer (not very popular on a campus of a theological seminary): you do not really have to know Hebrew or Greek to be able to understand the Scriptures. It's amazing how much of the Bible you can learn just by reading it in English. What I think the languages do is like the difference between a color photo and a black-and-white photo. Both the black and white and the color give you the picture, but one gives you a bit more depth, a bit more "color."

Philipp Melanchthon said, "The wisdom of the Bible is in the grammar." One of the reasons for knowing the languages is that when you are using commentaries, you discover that commentators are just like you. They're people who read the Bible and try to make sense out of it. The fact that they put their information in a book doesn't make them any more authoritative than you sitting in your study. When you get three or four commentaries, you discover that they differ. Usually commentators differ not because one bunch fell off a turnip truck and the other went to seminary. They differ because in order to translate the Bible, in order to comment on it, you have to try to understand its flow of thought. So as a preacher, you have to make interpretive decisions. For example, you have a subjective genitive, "The love of Christ constrains us." You ask, is that an objective genitive? Is that my love for Christ, or is it his love for me? You have to make a decision. In making that decision, it turns around and makes the rest of your passage and sermon. Read three or four translations and see where they are the same and where they differ. To be sure, it helps to know something of the language, to know why some translators didn't translate this passage in exactly the same way. So even if you only have a minimum knowledge of the language, you discover that it's a help. You can understand the translations, and you sometimes have a better understanding of the commentator.

But there is another reason that an exposure to the languages of the Bible can help you. Language not only is a way of expressing thought; language is a way of helping us think. We can't think apart from language. Benjamin Lee Whorf was a noted linguist who worked with the Hopi Indians in the American Southwest. As he worked with them, he discovered that they understood Einstein's theory of relativity. When it was explained to them, it made sense because in the Hopi language there is no sense of time. Hopis do not talk about the past, the present, the future. For them, everything is either happening here where they are or away from them; it has nothing to do with time.

For us, we cannot think apart from time if all we know is English. Bound up into English, and Greek for that matter, there is past, there is present, there is future, there is past beyond past; you just can't talk apart from time. Einstein said that he could not have thought of the theory of relativity if he did not understand mathematics and German. What Benjamin Lee Whorf came to realize was that language not only expresses thought; it also forms thought.

For instance, the Eskimos do not have merely a single word for snow—they have seventeen. They have words for snow falling, snow that has just hit the ground, snow that's beginning to freeze, snow that's been there for several days, snow that's beginning to melt. When Eskimos think of snow, they can really think of snow![3] Likewise, we do not have a single word for a bread product made from wheat. When we think of bread, we tend to think of a loaf of bread. We don't think of Twinkies or donuts or bear claws. In other parts of the world, that isn't so. Where people do not use wheat, one word may cover it all. So one advantage of knowing the language of the Bible, in particular, is that it enables you to understand how people thought in the ancient world.

That's what grammar is. It's the way people put their thought together. If you studied German, you'd know that the verb is in either the second position or the last position. Imagine how it is when you've got one of these long, complicated sentences and you have to wait until that final verb to discover what the action is. Grammar is that way. Those who study other languages often discover that you learn English by studying Greek. You grew up knowing English—you didn't know indirect objects or objects or prepositional phrases. These are ways of thinking. They're ways in which people put thought together.

So, to know the world of the Bible, it helps to know the history and the language that exposes us to the way the people in the ancient world thought.

### Culture

To know the Bible is to know its culture. It was only a few years ago that it dawned on me that the biblical writers and the readers were bound up in their culture. I used to think that the cultural problem of the Bible was that Paul said to greet one another with a holy kiss and we make it a hearty handshake. We don't want to go around kissing people in our churches. That makes sense. The more I work with it, as the revelation comes to us in Greek and Hebrew, it still comes to us out of a culture. That culture is all-pervasive. One of the enormous problems that you have as you work with the Bible is to understand how much of it is bound up in the culture and how much of it transcends culture. The answer is, all of it is bound up in the culture. It is out of that culture that you are to find the truth that transcends culture.

When I was broadcasting on *Discover the Word*, we were studying the book of Proverbs. If there's any book in the Old Testament that looks like a slam dunk, it's the book of Proverbs. Wisdom literature tends to move over from one culture to another with ease. But as you read that book and work with it, you find that in the last chapters the wisdom that is given is for young men who are preparing to serve in the king's court. There's a great deal about kings and royalty that you take for granted as you read the book. You ask

3. John B. Carroll, ed., *Language, Thought, and Reality: Selected Writings of Benjamin Lee Whorf* (Cambridge: MIT Press, 1956), 98, 216.

questions like, When the biblical writer talks about kings, is he saying that a monarchy is a preferred form of government?

Or consider the warnings in the book of Proverbs about cosigning a note. If you cosign, you cannot get out of it. You might beg, plead, nag—anything to get out of the obligation. The reason, of course, was that if you cosigned a note, you became responsible for the note. If the person who took the note out couldn't pay the note, the lender would come back to you, the cosigner. He could take you and everything you possess—your wife, your children—and sell them into slavery to pay off that note. If you cosigned a note, you were in big trouble in the ancient world. That's not true today. Today you can file for Chapter 11 bankruptcy. The fuss in Proverbs about cosigning a note, while probably still a good thing to keep in mind, doesn't cause the same alarm today as it did in the ancient world. The question is, What do you bring over to the twenty-first century? With what force do you bring it over to today?

When you're dealing with the ancient world of the Bible, you have to know its language, you have to know its history, you have to know its culture.

The danger at this point is that there are preachers who never get out of the ancient world. All of their preaching is at least two thousand years old or more. What they deal with in their sermons is the language, the history, the culture of the ancient world from which the Bible comes. Those are the kinds of sermons from which you leave saying, "David shouldn't have done that with Bathsheba" or "Abraham made a mistake when he went down to Egypt," but it doesn't touch today. A person who takes the Bible seriously understands the ancient world.

## The Second World: The Modern World

### History

The world of the preacher, the modern world, is the world that I have to work with—the world of homiletics, the world of the twenty-first century. This world, too, has a history. Evangelicals, it seems to me, have a tendency to ignore history. Unfortunately, history will not ignore us. We might want to ignore history, but history does not ignore us.

I remember the first time I ever talked with someone, a couple, considering an abortion. It was in the middle sixties and I was working with a group of physicians in Dallas in a Bible study. The young man and his wife came to my office. He was in his third year of medical school. They discovered that his wife was pregnant, which, to them, got in the way of their plans. She had been working to put him through school, and it looked like that would change. He was going to go on to advanced residency, and that was going to take several years, and children were not in their plans. They came to tell me that they were seriously thinking, in light of their situation, of having an abortion. That was 1965. I can still remember the feelings that I had. If they had told me that they had a two-year-old and that they were going to kill the two-year-old because he was just getting on their nerves, I might have understood that! But I couldn't have been more repulsed by the thought of abortion. I did not know how to handle it.

In 1968 there was the first of a number of judicial decisions related to abortion. Up until that time in our country, every state in the union had laws against abortion. Two—Colorado and Hawaii—allowed abortion if a woman's health was affected. Then in 1973 when *Roe v. Wade* was upheld by the Supreme Court, abortion became the law of the land. Today a million or more pre-borns are aborted. Numerous women in our society have had an abortion. If you don't keep that in mind as you get up to thunder like a prophet against the evils of abortion and recognize that in front of you in that congregation are a group of women who have had an abortion, you cut their hearts out and bring back a whole flood of guilt. You can't be just a prophet today; you have to be a pastor. You have to understand that history has caught up with you. We ignore history, but it doesn't ignore us.

I would like to believe that the reason folks today, more or less, think it's good to have churches that are racially integrated is because a group of theologians from Gordon-Conwell and Trinity and Dallas and Fuller and Westminster got together in the 1940s and studied the book of Ephesians. One of them might have said, "You know, the middle wall was broken down between the Jews and the gentiles. It strikes me that that must have some in-fluence, some effect on blacks and whites. We ought to break down the wall in our churches." It didn't happen that way. Rosa Parks got tired of sitting in the back of the bus and didn't move. And then there were the marchers of the 1950s and 1960s. The last group to figure it all out were the churches, and some haven't figured it out yet. Integration didn't come because we were so biblically correct and so formed by the Scriptures that we said, "This has got to go! It's damnable; it's against the law of Christ!" No, it happened out there on the streets. We ignore history, but it doesn't ignore us.

We have the issues of pollution, poverty, and the defiling of our environ-ment, among many others. Have we talked about them at all? Do we think about them? I remember talking to a Catholic priest who told me that part of his responsibility was to hear confessions from nuns. I asked him what that was like. He said it was like being stoned to death with popcorn. I grew up in a church that knew the will of God for the length of a person's hair and whether you should wear a beard and how long or short a woman's dress length should be, but the church never ever talked about segregation, integration, or the issues that were tearing at our society. You can ignore history, but it won't ignore you. It keeps knocking on the door and saying, "Look! Here's the agenda!" It's not wrong if society sets the agenda, but it demands that we answer it. You can ignore it, but it won't ignore you.

### Language

We also have a language of the twenty-first century. It's the language of the communicator, the language of the preacher. It is the language of the marketplace. It's the language of the Volkswagen ad. It's the vernacular, it's the common language, the *koine* in Greek. Somehow, when we get into church, we lose that accent. The preacher stands up on a Sunday morning, "Oh, God, Thou who sittest on the rim of the universe, we come to you with all of our humility and ask you . . ." You can imagine what happens if that man, after the service is over, goes to the local McDonald's and says (in a preaching tone of voice), "I'd like three hamburgers, two Cokes, and an order of French fries. And be thou quick about it." People would think he had lost his mind. When we do that in church, to the ear of the person who hasn't been there for fifteen years this kind of language sounds like it came from another planet—or certainly from another era.

The language of the communicator is the language of the people on the street. It's that language at its best. To fail to recognize that is to bathe the message of the gospel in the Bible in an antiquity that makes it sound, by the way we speak it, that it is irrelevant to people today.

### Culture

When I think of culture, I think of colored paper over people's eyes. Those of us in the United States may have blue paper. The folks in Latin America may have yellow paper. People from Europe, from England, may have orange paper. When we look through that paper, we all see the same thing but differently. In fact, that paper is so prevalent, it never goes away, so that you cannot imagine that anyone else can see anything differently than the way you see it. That's the culture coloring what we see. We're so caught in the culture, it's hard to step outside and evaluate it.

Look at what it is like to grow up in this culture. How do you preach the lordship of Christ in a democracy? Once every four years, the candidates for the office of the president of the United States come to us and beg for our vote. Every two years members of Congress come back to us and want us to give them our vote. Every six years the senators are around, wanting the vote. We vote them in, we vote them out. How do you preach the lordship of Christ in a democracy? If I understand the book of Acts and the rest of the New Testament, God isn't asking for our vote. Some people's view of an election is that if God votes yes and Satan votes no, we cast the deciding vote. We see it in our vocabulary. We say, "Make Jesus Christ Lord of your life." But that's not good theology. You don't make him Lord. He's not running for office. The New Testament says that he *is* Lord, like the fact that gravity is a law. And if you do not respond to that, you'll go to hell.

Likewise, in our culture how do you preach grace? One of the themes of modern advertising is that whatever you get, you deserve. You can see it in car ads. It's dark, and there's one light on up in the fifth story of the office building. The voice-over says, "You've worked hard to get to the top. You've given it your best effort. Now you've achieved, now you have the prize of victory." The light goes out. This man walks out with his briefcase and gets into a brand-new Cadillac or BMW or Buick. You know why you have a car like that? Not to get from point A to point B. You have a BMW or a Buick because this is a way of putting your neighbor in your exhaust fumes. You deserved it. This is the symbol of your victory. That's true with hamburgers. You go to a McDonald's why? Because, as their ad states, "You deserve a break today." If everything you get, from automobiles to hamburgers, is something you deserve, how in the world do you ever preach grace?

No wonder pastors have people say to them, "I'm angry with God." "Oh?" you ask. "I'm not just angry with him. I'm upset with God," the person says. You want to say, but you don't, "Do you know that every drop of water that you get this side of hell is sheer grace? He doesn't owe you anything. He owns you; he doesn't owe you." The tricky thing is, you can't say that in this culture. You can say it, but people don't hear it. Or if they hear it, they walk away angry at God—and you. You preach in this culture. How do you do it?

How do you preach in a culture that's dominated by images? The average person watches television twenty-six hours a week, not to mention the time that's spent on the computer or on the smartphone. Before beginning school, a child spends six thousand hours in front of a television set. From the time they go to school until the time they graduate, they spend another seventeen thousand or more hours in front of the television set or some other media device. By the time somebody gets to be twenty years of age, they will have watched seven hundred thousand commercials—all of them designed to sell, all of them fast, all of them moving, all of them image, all of them touching emotion. You may come to the pulpit with a sermon that sounds like a classroom lecture. They end up not listening. You think, "They should listen!"

But they don't. If you're going to communicate with this world, you've got to take these things into account. You may despise it, you may preach against it, you may not like it, but it's the way it is. These are the people who come to you in that culture, out of that culture; you're part of that culture, and you can't avoid it. Analyze it all you want, and when you're all through, if you're going to touch this generation for God, you touch them within their culture.

## The Third World: The World of the Preacher's Listeners

### History

This world is a particular world. This is the church with the zip code. This is the church at Fifth and Main. This is where *you* minister. This is the Bible class *you* have, the Sunday school class *you* teach. It is part of this modern world, but in a sense, it is more particular than that. It, too, has a history. That history has shaped those people.

When I was teaching at Dallas Seminary in our Department of Pastoral Ministry in the early 1970s, we had a project that students were assigned to do. One of the students wanted to do a history of his church. He had just become the pastor of a Baptist church in a little East Texas town, and he thought it would be nice to do the history. He'd wanted to go back at least seventy-five years and see how this church had developed. He discovered that in the 1950s there was a young black man in town who was accused of raping a white woman. A vigilante group got hold of him, set up a cross on the lawn of that church, and burned him to death. In the 1960s, for other reasons, apparently, the church split. I mean *split*. When a church in a small town splits, everything splits—families split, businesses in town are affected, the whole community is affected. In big cities, you can go from one church to another. In a small town when you split, you've got problems. He discovered several similar issues. When he went door-to-door inviting people to come to First Baptist Church, he discovered that the community remembered a burning cross on the lawn, and they could feel the effect a split had had in their family. This newly minted preacher was simply trying to do something for God. He found out that there was a lot of history to that church. Your people have a history.

### Language

You preach to people out of a history. You preach to people in their particular language. There's a language used in the Northeast, a language that is used in the South, a language used in Harlem, where I grew up. It's not a language that you put on; you know it.

When I was serving in Denver, we had a man from Great Britain who came as a student. He was trying to relate to an American audience. He talked about a baseball game and was serious when he said, "The man ended the game by getting a four-base hit." We knew what he meant, but we also knew that he didn't know baseball. You have a single, a double—but a four-base hit? No, it's a home run! As listeners we didn't sit and turn down the volume and remark to each other, "That's the last we'll listen to him!" We knew he wasn't from here. But that's possibly why some people can preach in one situation and can't make it in another. Know the language.

## Culture

I went on a preaching engagement in Aurora, Nebraska. It's not the end of the earth, but if you got on a tall building you could see the end of the earth from Aurora. I remember going to the town and going to their little motel and wondering how I got there. Why did I say yes to this? Then I opened my folder and they had on the stationery, "The Greater Nebraska Crusade for Christ." I thought sarcastically, we're going to get all of Nebraska together—all ten of them—and we're going to have an evangelistic crusade. Nevertheless, I came prepared to preach the gospel.

I discovered that there were three churches in town that sponsored the event, which was really a Bible conference in the local high school. I asked the man who invited me about the stationery. He said that back in the 1950s they had had Marv Rosell, the father of professor Garth Rosell of Gordon-Conwell Theological Seminary, for an evangelistic crusade. At that time they had invested in the stationery and didn't want to waste it! I was invited and so I went.

It was a different world. When you turn on the television in Aurora, Nebraska, early on is a weather report. The weather report comes between the news and sports. They also had a report from the Chicago livestock, produce, and grain markets. When I was in Denver, I used to get up about 5:15 a.m., and about 5:25 a.m. came the farm report. I was there twelve years and heard it every morning, and I still don't understand the farm report. In Aurora, Nebraska, the weather report is more important than the ball scores. Anybody who ministers in Aurora understands those market reports, understands the weather.

One of the graduates from Denver Seminary went to Wyoming to serve as a pastor. He has a church with 275 to 300 people in a town that has about

200 people. You talk about mega-church, that's mega-church up in Wyoming. He said,

> There are certain times of the year that my worst nightmare would be that you would show up for church, and I would have to preach. When it comes to harvest time, I get out with the folks of the church and help to bring in the harvest. I work the tractor, and sometimes I get an hour and a half to prepare for preaching, if I have that. Some of those sermons I preach are simply terrible. But I know that at that time of year, it's more important for me to be out there than to be preparing in my study.

I spent some time with him. In the morning from about seven to nine o'clock he'd sit in the only restaurant in town, and the whole town would come in. He knew all about his people and understood them: "How's that new calf doing? How's the wife doing? You going to get that crop in?" He understood how to work a town in Wyoming.

You minister in a particular place. You speak the language, you know the culture, you're aware of the history. There are some of God's great saints who can minister in Aurora, Nebraska, when someone like myself couldn't touch the place. You have a culture and background, and so does the place you're in.

## The Fourth World: The World of the Preacher

There's one other world, and it's the one that's easiest to overlook: your world. Sure, it's easy to look at the world of the Bible and the modern world and the world in which I live. But there's a way in which I'm in the middle of all these worlds. That is, when I study the ancient texts, *I* study the ancient texts. One of the insights from scholars in literature studies is that there is a distance between myself and that text. There is some meaning that comes between myself and the text, and I can't avoid that. While I believe with all my heart in authorial intent, I also recognize that when I study the text, *I* study it. You'll see something in the text that I won't see. Because you're the one interpreting it, you will interpret it differently than I will. You come out of this modern world with your own background, your own experiences of growing up. You've got a way of talking, a way of thinking, a way of handling life. You're you, for better or worse; for richer or poorer, you're you.

A lot of people, for example, go into ministry because they grew up in dysfunctional families and are trying to fix either themselves or others. That's the wrong reason to go into ministry. They may even come from perfectionistic families. If you grew up in a perfectionistic family, you could never please your parents, even dad. You'd get three As and a B and dad would say, "How come you didn't get four As?" Then you'd work hard and get four As and your folks would respond, "Must be something wrong with the school system if you can get four As that easily!"

One of the marks of those kinds of preachers is that they get into churches as angry people. You can see it in the way they preach. One of their major moods in preaching is guilt. There are people who take any passage in the Bible and turn it into a guilt trip. The reason is that they feel guilty. All their lives they've not been able to measure up. They have a difficult time praising their congregation. They have a hard time praising their kids. It would be all they could do to sit down with their daughter or son and say, "You know, you're great. The greatest thing that ever happened to me was to have you. I want you to know that you're a first-class winner. You're great! You're really something!" Some people can't do it. This makes it difficult for you to encourage your kids. If that's true of you, you're going to find it hard to praise a congregation. We then turn every sermon into guilt.

Take a passage like 1 Peter 1:3–5: "Praise be to the God and Father of our Lord Jesus Christ! In his great mercy he has given us new birth into a living hope through the resurrection of Jesus Christ from the dead, and into an inheritance that can never perish, spoil or fade. This inheritance is kept in heaven for you, who through faith are shielded by God's power." That's brimming with hope! That's optimism! You can't beat that. Except when an angry preacher gets ahold of it and says, "You don't have that hope, do you? You don't live in that hope." Therefore, every week people come to church, and you set the bar, and they jump. The next week they come back, and they think they've jumped high enough, but no, the bar is higher still. They can't please the pastor, and then they figure they can't ever please God.

There are two doctrines that hold me. I grew up in New York City in a tough, hard area—in the section of Harlem called Mousetown. *Reader's Digest* said it was the toughest place in the United States—an area known for its viciousness, its vice, its violence.[4] Two doctrines hold me. One is that I believe in depravity. I think it is the best-proved doctrine of the Christian faith. I think all of us suffer from a curvature of the soul. All of us have polluted bloodstreams. Whenever I get into a discussion with somebody who tells me that everybody is inherently good, I can hardly continue the discussion. Have you ever been in a discussion with somebody who honestly believes the earth is flat? You say, "What about the astronauts? They went around . . ."

4. Bradford Chambers, "Boy Gangs of Mousetown," *Reader's Digest* 53 (August 1948): 144–58.

"Oh, no, no." This person's got every answer. Like the folks who believe in UFOs—they simply believe in them. Nothing you say works. The people who believe that men and women are inherently good, I don't know how to handle them. We all suffer from a curvature of the soul. I believe that. I believe in the doctrine of depravity.

I also believe in the grace of God. I believe that to the core of my being. I believe in grace; I believe in depravity. Those are not the only two doctrines from the Christian faith. I need other Christians who are aware of sovereignty and of righteousness. I need them. I need to be reminded that God is more than that. But for me, grace and depravity anchor my soul.

What we are we bring to our study, we bring to our preaching. People in the congregation who are with you several years begin to become like you. For better or worse, richer or poorer, that's what happens. So you've got to ask yourself, "Who am I when I preach? Am I a prophet? Am I a drill sergeant? Am I a teacher? Am I a counselor? Am I a shepherd?" You better define what you mean by "shepherd." That's an image that gets lost in the twenty-first century. "Who am I?" The answer to that question is often shaped by who you are when you move into ministry, understanding your history, language, and culture.

## Conclusion

These are the four worlds of the preacher: the Bible, the preacher in the modern world, the preacher's world of ministry, and the preacher's personal world. To live in these worlds, you need to know the history, the language, and the culture of each world. You come away from reading this overview and you may say, "Who is sufficient to preach in this complex and layered world?" The answer is: none of us. With all the flaws that we have, somehow God uses us in this big, wide world through these four worlds—to his glory.

# 2

## The Preacher and the World of the Old Testament

STEVEN D. MATHEWSON

### Introduction

Preaching from the Old Testament resembles playing the saxophone. It is easy to do poorly.[1] But over the years, Haddon Robinson did it well. His skill in preaching the Bible Jesus read influenced my decision to seek him out as a mentor.[2] He was a remarkable mentor and friend, and I am honored to contribute this chapter as a way of honoring him.

Why did Haddon handle the Old Testament so well in his preaching? Perhaps it was because he chose his friends wisely. He was a close friend of Bruce Waltke, a giant in evangelical Old Testament scholarship. Or perhaps it is because he read works that many preachers ignore. For example, Haddon interacted deeply with Robert Alter's *The Art of Biblical Narrative* before it was fashionable to do so.

I suspect, though, that Haddon's skill flowed from his commitment to the "four worlds of the preacher," which he articulated so carefully. In honor

---

1. This is one of the many metaphors I have borrowed after first hearing it used by Haddon Robinson.

2. This way of describing the Old Testament comes from the title of a book by Philip Yancey: *The Bible Jesus Read* (Grand Rapids: Zondervan, 1999).

of my esteemed mentor, I will address four aspects preachers must consider when they enter the world of the Old Testament to preach it effectively to their congregations. These four aspects roughly correspond to Robinson's four worlds of the preacher.

## The Text of the Old Testament

The first world Robinson discusses in his lecture is the world of the Bible. God has given us a written text that we must understand if we are going to understand his thoughts. This requires attention to two particular aspects of the Old Testament text: its language and its literary genres.

### The Language of the Old Testament

Robinson begins his discussion of the biblical languages with a disclaimer: you do not really have to know Hebrew or Greek to be able to understand the Scriptures (see chap. 1). Yet, he observes, reading the Bible in its original languages provides color, depth, and a more precise understanding of how the biblical writers expressed their thoughts.

I remember the first time I read through Psalm 23 in the Hebrew Bible and came to verse 6. A couple words leaped off the page and startled me. The first was the verb *radaph*. I had grown accustomed to the language of the King James Version, which virtually every translation has since adopted: "Surely goodness and mercy shall follow me all the days of my life." Yet the term "follow" was not one of the meanings ascribed to this verb on my Hebrew vocabulary cards. The term *radaph* meant "to pursue, chase, persecute." It struck me how God's goodness and mercy was pursuing or chasing after me. It was hunting me down! Then I discovered the word *ḥesed*—"loyal love." *Surely goodness and loyal love will pursue me all the days of my life*. That's the living color provided by reading the text in its original language.

Similarly, I remember discovering how the *wayyiqtol* verbs in Hebrew narrative advance the main line of a story, while a *qatal* form has the effect of pausing the action and adding some kind of commentary or insight before the story line is resumed.[3] For example, after a string of *wayyiqtol* verbs in Genesis 38:14, the narrator pauses the action with three *qatal* forms. This pause gives insight into why Tamar took off her widow's clothes, put on a

---

3. Steven D. Mathewson, *The Art of Preaching Old Testament Narrative* (Grand Rapids: Baker Academic, 2002), 231–32.

veil, and sat along the route her father-in-law, Judah, was traveling: she saw that Judah had no intention of giving his son, Shelah, to her as a husband.

More recently, I have noticed that constructions in which the Hebrew verb "to see" (*ra'ah*) is followed by "that" (*ki*) introduce a condition. These instances do not emphasize the physical perception of an object or an event. Rather, they portray the realization of a state of affairs.

These kinds of insights make it worthwhile for pastors to learn and maintain their Hebrew. Or do they? The fact is, few pastors leave seminary with confidence in their ability to read and study the Hebrew Bible. Add to this the demands of pastoral ministry, and it is fair to ask whether it is really worth investing so much time and effort to attain a beginner's-level understanding of the language. I believe it is. First, the fact that you cannot read the Hebrew Bible with the proficiency of your Hebrew professors may work in your favor. As one of my Hebrew professors used to say, this forces you to go through the text more slowly. Furthermore, if you are going to devote your life to proclaiming a particular document (in this case, the Bible), does it not make sense to learn the languages in which that document was written?

The circumstances have never been better for pastors who want to maintain or resuscitate their knowledge of biblical Hebrew. Software programs like *BibleWorks* and *Logos* allow for instant definitions and parsing of each word. The *Lexham Discourse Hebrew Bible* in *Logos* gives users access to an instant linguistic analysis of the Old Testament text.

My suggestion is to devote an initial hour of sermon preparation time to the study of the biblical text in its original languages. If you are preaching on Psalm 121 (8 verses) or Deuteronomy 6:4–9, you can likely work through the entire text in Hebrew. If you are preaching 1 Samuel 17 (58 verses) or Ecclesiastes 3 (22 verses), you will need to concentrate on a few key verses that you want to look at more closely. Do this on day one of your sermon preparation—before you turn to the commentaries. Then, on each successive day, go back and review the key verses or passages in the Hebrew text.

When you're preaching from the New Testament and (hopefully) working in the Greek text, you can still discipline yourself to read from the Hebrew Bible for ten minutes a day. Don't stop for detailed analysis. Simply read the text with the help of your Bible software programs. Read through a book you'll eventually preach. Or read and meditate on one proverb a day from the book of Proverbs.

It will be tempting to sprinkle comments about Hebrew words or grammatical construction into your sermon. Avoid this as much as possible. Simply look at your study of the Hebrew text as the homework that gives you confidence to make some simple yet profound insights. For example, you might say, "In Psalm 23:6, the word translated 'follow' had the idea in David's time of pursuing something or chasing someone down." No reference to Hebrew is needed.

Finally, I have read and studied the Hebrew Bible for more than three decades, yet I am average at best. That is okay. I still benefit from it. As a colleague used to say, "Use what you've got, and don't obsess over what you are not." Knowing only a bit of Hebrew can make you dangerous if you are not humble. Besides, it is just as easy to disobey the Bible in Hebrew as it is to disobey it in English. But using whatever level of Hebrew you have will enable you, if nothing else, to carry on a conversation with those commentators who read Hebrew like you read English. The end result will be a clearer, more exact understanding of the Old Testament.

### The Literary Genres of the Old Testament

For years, Haddon Robinson required his doctoral students in preaching to read *How to Read the Bible for All Its Worth* by Gordon D. Fee and Douglas Stuart.[4] This reflects his conviction that we cannot fully understand the message of a text unless we understand the genre (type of literature) in which it was communicated. For example, the narrative of the sea-crossing in Exodus 14 communicates its message differently than does the song (psalm) of Moses and Miriam in Exodus 15. The case laws in Exodus 21 take an entirely different approach.

Paying attention to the various literary genres found in the Old Testament contributes something else besides a rich understanding of the text. It also helps with communication. One of the complaints I hear most frequently from listeners is that the sermons they hear from their pastors week after week sound the same. That is, they lack variety. They are stale, not fresh. In most cases, these listeners are receptive to Scripture and are not looking to be amused. They have simply grown tired of the same sermon form or approach week after week. Living in a media-saturated, communications-savvy culture only exacerbates this problem. So what is the solution? Robinson argues: "To actually preach with variety and excitement, we must treat the Scriptures as they are—a library of different types of literature."[5]

The challenge, then, is to reflect this variety in the shape and style of our sermons. Other homileticians agree. Fred Craddock has asked, "Why should

4. Gordon D. Fee and Douglas Stuart, *How to Read the Bible for All Its Worth*, 4th ed. (Grand Rapids: Zondervan, 2014).
5. Haddon W. Robinson, foreword to *Preaching with Variety*, by Jeffrey D. Arthurs (Grand Rapids: Kregel, 2007), 11.

the multitude of forms and moods within biblical literature . . . be brought together in one unvarying mold, and that copied from Greek rhetoricians of centuries ago?"[6] Similarly, Don Wardlaw argues, "When preachers feel they have not preached a passage of Scripture unless they have dissected and rearranged that Word into a lawyer's brief, they in reality make the Word of God subservient to one particular, technical kind of reason."[7]

This does not mean preachers will speak in parallel lines of poetry when preaching Psalm 46 or will simply tell a story when preaching 1 Samuel 17. Instead, Jeffrey Arthurs calls preachers to reproduce or re-create the rhetorical dynamics of the literary genres from which they are heralding the Word of God.[8] A couple of examples will have to suffice. I have written elsewhere on Old Testament narrative,[9] so I'll focus here on Old Testament poetry.

A sermon on a poetic text must invite listeners to savor its imagery and rhetorical effects. Expressions like "notice the three characteristics of God's protection" should give way to "what a beautiful picture of God's protection" or "this picture of God's protection makes us feel secure." When preaching Ecclesiastes 1, ask your listeners to imagine the sun panting (the idea of the Hebrew verb typically translated as "hurries" or "hastens") as it runs back to the eastern horizon during the night to get ready for another day of rising and setting. Also, be cautious about technical jargon. I never refer to the "synonymous" or "antithetical" parallelism in a psalm. Instead, I will say that a particular verse seems to present its message "in surround sound like you experience at a movie theater."

When preaching the Wisdom literature of the Old Testament, Arthurs suggests crafting the sermon's big idea as a proverb and making a biblical proverb duel with a worldly proverb.[10] Proverbs 10:9 says:

> Whoever walks in integrity walks securely,
>   but whoever takes crooked paths will be found out.

I have contrasted this with the popular saying, "What happens in Vegas stays in Vegas." No, it does not. Sinful behavior comes back to haunt you.

---

6. Fred B. Craddock, *As One without Authority* (Nashville: Abingdon, 1971), 143–44.

7. Don M. Wardlaw, "Introduction: The Need for New Shapes," in *Preaching Biblically*, ed. Don M. Wardlaw (Philadelphia: Westminster, 1983), 16.

8. Arthurs, *Preaching with Variety*, 13.

9. In addition to *The Art of Preaching Old Testament Narrative*, see my further thinking about this topic in Steven D. Mathewson, "Prophetic Preaching from the Old Testament," in *Text Message: The Centrality of Scripture in Preaching*, ed. Ian Stackhouse and Oliver Crisp (Eugene, OR: Wipf and Stock, 2014), 34–53.

10. Arthurs, *Preaching with Variety*, 150.

When we preach, we cannot reproduce the form in which an Old Testament text was written. But we can re-create its effects. As Warren Wiersbe says, "To preach biblically means much more than to preach the truth of the Bible accurately. It also means to present that truth the way the biblical writers and speakers presented it."[11]

## The Culture of the Old Testament

One of my favorite museums to visit in Chicago has free admission. Yet the experience is priceless. The Oriental Institute Museum on the campus of the University of Chicago houses artifacts connected to the people, places, and events recorded in the Old Testament. Visitors can walk past two of the colorful striding lions that the prophet Daniel would have walked by when leaving the ancient city of Babylon via the Processional Way. Visitors can also see Sennacherib's Prism—a six-sided clay prism on which the Assyrian king described eight military campaigns, including his siege of Jerusalem, which the Old Testament describes in 2 Kings 18–19; 2 Chronicles 32; and Isaiah 36–37.

I love this museum for the way it helps me understand the second world to which preachers must pay attention: the culture of the Old Testament. The Old Testament was not a word delivered from outer space.[12] Rather, its human authors lived and wrote in a particular historical-cultural context. Of course, our listeners want answers to life's pressing questions, not an excursus on the military practices of the Assyrians or the religion of the Babylonians. But if we are going to reveal the living God through our preaching, we must understand the culture behind the text. There are two aspects that deserve our consideration: people and geography. These may be as or more important than understanding biblical Hebrew.

### Old Testament People and Their Customs

Psalm 87 demonstrates the importance of knowing something about the nations surrounding Israel. The psalm sings the praises of Zion, God's holy city. Verse 4 summarizes the "glorious things" said about the city of God:

11. Warren W. Wiersbe, *Preaching and Teaching with Imagination: The Quest for Biblical Ministry* (Wheaton: Victor, 1994), 36.
12. Kevin Vanhoozer made this observation about Scripture as inspired discourse during a lecture titled "Inerrancy and Hermeneutics" (Lecture, Evangelical Free Church of America Theology Conference, Trinity International University, Deerfield, IL, January 29, 2015), available at https://go.efca.org/resources/document/2015-efca-theology-conference-resources.

> I will record Rahab and Babylon
>     among those who acknowledge me—
> Philistia too, and Tyre, along with Cush—
>     and will say, "This one was born in Zion."

Readers who lack knowledge of the peoples in the world of the Old Testament will respond tepidly to this verse. But it will stun those who understand that Rahab (Egypt), Babylon, and Philistia were bitter enemies of Israel and had their own gods and goddesses. What a shock to hear God speaking of these nations with terms of endearment and even describing them as Zion-born! Without an understanding of these nations, we will fail to appreciate the wonder of that future day when people from these nations will find their spiritual home in Zion.[13]

Sometimes the religious customs of Israel's neighbors shed light on the meaning of a text. How can we preach 1 Kings 18 and describe Elijah's confrontation with the prophets of Baal without knowing something about Canaanite religion? The Epic of Baal, discovered at the ancient city of Ugarit, portrays the storm god, Baal, as the one who produces rain and causes lightning and thunder. Baal's ongoing struggle against the god of the underworld, Mot, evokes the autumn rains coming off of the Mediterranean Sea.[14] The confrontation on Mount Carmel will reveal, then, who controls the rain and the fire. Lissa Wray Beal also comments: "The taunt about the journey or Baal's slumber [v. 27] snidely uses the myth of Baal's yearly descent to the underworld of Mot where he is held powerless until the growing season begins. Elijah mocks that Baal's inability to return or answer from his underworld imprisonment shows he is no god at all."[15]

Even the customs of everyday life shed light on Old Testament texts. Whenever I preach Genesis 38, I point out that Tamar's request for Judah to leave his seal and staff was the ancient equivalent of asking for his driver's license and a major credit card. The engraving on a lip-balm–sized cylinder seal created the marks of personal identification.[16] Furthermore, I help listeners understand the joy described in Isaiah 9:3–5 over Israel's deliverance from military oppression by briefly describing the brutality of the Assyrian army.

13. See Tremper Longman III, *Psalms*, Tyndale Old Testament Commentaries (Downers Grove, IL: InterVarsity, 2014), 319.

14. Mark Smith, "The Baal Cycle," in *Ugaritic Narrative Poetry*, ed. Simon B. Parker (Atlanta: Scholars Press, 1997), 81–86.

15. Lissa M. Wray Beal, *1 and 2 Kings*, Apollos Old Testament Commentary (Downers Grove, IL: InterVarsity, 2014), 244.

16. Steven D. Mathewson, "An Exegetical Study of Genesis 38," *Bibliotheca Sacra* 146 (October–December 1989): 379.

Without dramatizing the gory details, I talk about how Sennacherib's palace in Nineveh contained scenes of his conquest of the Israelite city Lachish. These scenes portrayed the Assyrians impaling captives on poles and even flaying or dismembering others.[17]

### Old Testament Geography

Geographical insights can also shed light on a text's meaning. One of the most basic concepts to communicate to our listeners as we preach the Old Testament is the land of Israel as a "land bridge" between Egypt and Mesopotamia.[18] This geographical phenomenon helps us understand how the land could be both a blessing in times of obedience and a curse in times of disobedience. During Solomon's reign, the land served as a hub from which he could rule over the surrounding kingdoms and as a center for wisdom (see 1 Kings 4:20–34). Yet this same land bridge became a horrible buffer zone during conflicts between Egypt and Babylon. The godly king Josiah was killed while resisting the Egyptian army's march through the land of Israel on its way to help Assyria (2 Kings 23:29).

When preaching Isaiah 9:1–7, I always point out something I learned years ago from *The Macmillan Bible Atlas* (now *The Carta Bible Atlas*). The very areas God promised to honor—"Galilee of the nations, by the Way of the Sea, beyond the Jordan" (Isa. 9:1)—were the very areas ravaged by the Assyrian king Tiglath-pileser III in three successive campaigns from 734 to 732 BC.[19]

Similarly, a map with the location of the Philistine and Israelite forces as they prepare for the Battle of Gilboa suggests that King Saul snuck behind enemy lines to consult with the medium at Endor.[20] I mention this when preaching 1 Samuel 28 to show the severity of Saul's fear and desperation.

### A Strategy for Understanding Old Testament Culture

Once again, time is an issue when it comes to sermon preparation. But the right tools provide quick access to reliable historical-cultural information. For starters, preachers will do well to use the most recent exegetical commentaries. The latest edition of Tremper Longman III's *Old Testament*

---

17. Boyd Severs, *Warfare in the Old Testament* (Grand Rapids: Kregel, 2013), 239. See also Yigael Yadin, *The Art of Biblical Warfare*, vol. 2 (London: McGraw-Hill, 1963), 428–37.

18. See Anson F. Rainey and R. Steven Notley, *The Sacred Bridge: Carta's Atlas of the Biblical World*, 2nd ed. (Jerusalem: Carta Jerusalem, 2014), 30–42.

19. Yohanan Aharoni, Michael Avi-Yonah, Anson F. Rainey, and Ze'ev Safrai, *The Macmillan Bible Atlas*, 3rd rev. ed. (New York: Macmillan, 1993), 145–46.

20. Rainey and Notley, *Sacred Bridge*, 150.

*Commentary Survey* (Baker Academic) will give preachers good leads on the best commentaries for their sermon preparation. Preachers need to be cautious about using the free commentaries bundled with Bible software. These are typically older and out-of-date in terms of their historical-cultural insights.

Preachers need to add a good Bible dictionary or encyclopedia to their library. The six-volume *Anchor Bible Dictionary* (Bantam Doubleday Dell) has become a gold standard, although a one-volume work like the *New Bible Dictionary* (InterVarsity) will suffice. I have found Piotr Bienkowski and Allan Millard's affordable and concise *Dictionary of the Ancient Near East* (University of Pennsylvania) to be quite useful too.

There are other resources devoted solely to the historical-cultural background of the Bible. I often turn to *The IVP Bible Background Commentary: Old Testament* (IVP Academic) by John H. Walton, Victor H. Matthews, and Mark W. Chavalas. Another volume I regularly consult in my sermon preparation is *Life in Biblical Israel* by Philip J. King and Lawrence E. Stager (Westminster John Knox).

A good Bible atlas is also a necessity. I like *The Carta Bible Atlas* (Macmillan), noted above, since it maps just about every major event in the Bible. Other fine options include *The New Moody Atlas of the Bible* (Moody) by Barry J. Beitzel, *Zondervan Atlas of the Bible* (Zondervan) by Carl G. Rasmussen, and the *Crossway ESV Bible Atlas* (Crossway) by John D. Currid and David P. Barrett.

The above recommendations will grow out-of-date with time, but wise preachers will always stay alert to quality resources by Old Testament scholars for use in their sermon preparation. Likewise, they will sprinkle insights into their sermons subtly and creatively. Never say something like "let me give you some background information on ancient seals and staffs"—unless you want to anesthetize the minds of your listeners.

## Contemporary Culture and the Old Testament

The third world Haddon Robinson discusses in his lecture is the world of the preacher's listeners. He says that this is where *you* minister. It is the zip code in which your church exists. This context shapes the people to whom you preach, and it has an effect on the way that they hear or respond to your preaching from the Old Testament.

When I moved from zip code 59714 (a "rurban," or rural-urban, community in Montana) to 60048 (an affluent community on Chicago's North Shore), I discovered that my new listeners were not as enthusiastic about the narrative texts of the Old Testament as my previous congregation had been. Eventually, it dawned on me that a significant number of my listeners were scientists or engineers. They develop new pharmaceuticals or design cell phones. They figure out why bridges collapse and how to protect historic structures. So they tend to like the facts presented in a straightforward manner. I have not backed away from preaching Old Testament narrative, but I have worked harder to help them understand *how* narrative works and *why* we need to be patient with it.

However, while we must pay attention to our specific preaching context, I want to suggest strategies that cut across every zip code in the Western world. I am well aware that the city and suburbs of Portland (whether in Oregon or Maine) and Chicago are quite different. Yet there are moods or concerns or questions or values that span North America. As Eugene Peterson has observed, "The 'text' that seems to be most in favor on the American landscape today is the sovereign self."[21]

How then should the prevailing conditions in Western culture shape the way we preach the Old Testament? Iain Provan has recently suggested ten questions to pose to the Old Testament literature. He chose them "because they are precisely the kind that religions and philosophies have always tried to answer and about which we would expect any serious religious or philosophical literature to have something to say."[22] Personally, I find late moderns asking these questions and, in some cases, taking offense at the answers the Old Testament gives to them. In the brief survey that follows, I will offer some ways that preachers can address these questions as they preach the Old Testament.

### What Is the World?

The Old Testament begins with theology, not epistemology. "In the beginning God created the heavens and the earth" (Gen. 1:1). This theological declaration sets the stage for all that God will say throughout the Old Testament Scriptures. According to Provan, the book of Genesis reveals that "the order, goodness, and beauty that I find in the world as I first encounter it as a child are there to be found because the world is a creation of God, and it reflects his glory."[23] This means the world is neither eternal (as in Hinduism)

---

21. Eugene H. Peterson, *Eat This Book: A Conversation in the Art of Spiritual Reading* (Grand Rapids: Eerdmans, 2006), 16.

22. Iain Provan, *Seriously Dangerous Religion: What the Old Testament Really Says and Why It Matters* (Waco: Baylor University Press, 2014), 11–12.

23. Provan, *Seriously Dangerous Religion*, 46.

nor divine (as in pantheism). Yet the created world is a sacred space, created as a temple in which God's presence will dwell among his people.[24]

Our listeners need a theology of creation. Wise preachers will not settle for going into "apologetics mode" when they preach Genesis 1–2. Instead, they will proclaim its rich theology, which serves as a foundation for the rest of the Old Testament.

### Who Is God?

Late modern listeners need to hear from the Old Testament Scriptures that God is one (not many), sovereign, incomparable, all-present, and all-knowing. They also need to hear that God is good. Many suppose that the "Old Testament God" is not a benevolent being.

Over the years, I keep pointing listeners back to Exodus 34:5–7, the place where Yahweh shares his résumé after showing Moses the "afterburners" of his glory. When Moses says "show me your glory," Yahweh responds with "I will cause all my goodness to pass in front of you" (Exod. 33:18–19). According to Exodus 2:23–3:16, the name "Yahweh" signifies God's ongoing care for his people and his willingness to act on their behalf. Then, as his goodness passes in front of Moses, Yahweh proclaims himself in Exodus 34:5–7 as slow to anger and abounding in love.

It's important that we help our listeners understand God's anger in the context of his love. His anger is not the twisted rage surmised by the new atheists.[25] Rather, it is his measured, controlled, stunning response to evil. Without it, God would not be just. Furthermore, Exodus 34:5–7 mitigates the declaration of God's anger by surrounding it with affirmations of his love and by describing his anger as slow. The Hebrew in Exodus 34:6 is expressive, picturing God's nose as taking a long time to get red with anger. The themes of loyal love and faithfulness in Exodus 34:5–7 reverberate throughout the Old Testament, so preachers will do well to highlight them and trace them back to this moment.[26]

Another troubling detail that seems at odds with God's goodness is his sanctioning of "holy war." Here are a few observations that we may want to point out to our listeners when preaching the laws pertaining to *herem* ("ban") in Deuteronomy or the conquest narratives in Joshua.

24. Provan, *Seriously Dangerous Religion*, 32–40. See also John H. Walton, *Genesis*, The NIV Application Commentary (Grand Rapids: Zondervan, 2001), 147–48.

25. For example, see Christopher Hitchens, *God Is Not Great: How Religion Poisons Everything* (New York: Warner, 2007), 97–108.

26. See, e.g., Pss. 40:11; 57:3; 86:15; 89:14; 92:2; 100:5; 117:2; Prov. 3:3; Isa. 16:5; Lam. 3:22–23.

1. The expression "holy war" never appears in the Bible. Instead, the conquest stories refer to "a war in which the God of the Israelites won the victory over their enemies."[27]

2. Yahweh did not act out of nationalistic interests; in fact, he created Israel for the very purpose of blessing all families of the earth (Gen. 12:1–3).[28]

3. "The very first Canaanite we meet in the narrative of the Conquest of Canaan [Rahab] is a converted one who gets saved."[29] This story demonstrates Yahweh's love for people of other cultures and races who turn to him.[30]

4. The conquest of Canaan was a "unique and limited historical event" that was not continued and that was never intended to be a model for how future generations of God's people should treat their enemies.[31]

5. "Yahweh's aversion to evil prompted him to deal severely with his own people, Israel (Josh. 7; Judg. 2:14–15),"[32] so the conquest was rooted in God's justice and not any quest for ethnic cleansing—a practice fueled by racial hatred.[33]

### Who Are Man and Woman?

Recently, a grade-school teacher in the church I serve shared with me about a second grader who was transitioning from one gender to another—with full support of the parents. It is into this culture that preachers have the responsibility to proclaim what the Old Testament says about human beings and their sexuality.

The place to start, I suggest, is the creation of human beings in the image and likeness of God. Often, "image of God" gets defined as the ways in which human beings resemble their Creator. However, abundance of research suggests otherwise.[34] The term "likeness" certainly affirms that people resemble the One who created them. But in Genesis 1:26 when God says, "Let us make

---

27. Christopher J. H. Wright, *The God I Don't Understand: Reflections on Tough Questions of Faith* (Grand Rapids: Zondervan, 2008), 87. For example, see Josh. 10:42 and 23:3.

28. Steven D. Mathewson, *Joshua and Judges*, The People's Bible Commentary (Oxford: The Bible Reading Fellowship, 2003), 17.

29. Wright, *God I Don't Understand*, 101.

30. Mathewson, *Joshua and Judges*, 17.

31. Wright, *God I Don't Understand*, 90.

32. Mathewson, *Joshua and Judges*, 17.

33. Paul Copan, *Is God a Moral Monster? Making Sense of the Old Testament God* (Grand Rapids: Baker Books, 2011), 163.

34. See J. Richard Middleton, *The Liberating Image: The* Imago Dei *in Genesis 1* (Grand Rapids: Brazos, 2005), 43–90. Catherine L. McDowell makes this summary observation about "image of God" in Gen. 1:26–27: "The author seems to invite the comparison of humans to

mankind in our image," he is saying: "Let's make mankind as our representative on planet earth."

In the ancient Near East, a king who ruled a great empire faced the challenge of keeping subjects in more distant regions loyal to him. He couldn't give a "state of the empire address" on television or even distribute photographs of himself and the royal family. So how were his subjects six hundred miles away supposed to be in awe of him? The king would set up a statue in the remote provinces of his empire. These images were to serve as visible representatives of his invisible presence. In Daniel 3:1, the Babylonian king Nebuchadnezzar set up an image ninety feet high and nine feet wide for this purpose. Even kings were often referred to as "images of god." They were considered to be the visible representatives of a particular god, charged with the responsibility of carrying out the program of that god.

Preachers will do well to help listeners see the enormous implications of this for their lives. Creation in the image of God establishes the value of human life. This leads to a sense of wonder over human beings, and that wonder leads us to the worship of God (see Ps. 8). It leads us to treat others with dignity and to care for the most vulnerable in society—the unborn and the elderly (see Gen. 9:6, in which creation in the image of God serves as the basis for not taking the life of another human being).

Late modern listeners also need the Old Testament's vision for human beings as male and female. Genesis 2:24 expresses marriage as an implication of the way God created human beings as male and female. Marriage is a lasting union between a man and a woman. This explains God's opposition throughout the Old Testament to divorce (though not to divorced people per se). It also explains the Old Testament's condemnation of same-sex activity (see Lev. 18:22; 20:13).

### Why Do Evil and Suffering Mark the World?

The problem of evil perplexes late modern listeners just as it has troubled people throughout the ages. The question usually gets framed like this: If there is a God, then why is there cancer and mental illness and sexual abuse and genocide and terrorism? The short answer is that, three chapters into the Old Testament's story, the rebellion of the first human beings results in evil entering the world. Provan makes two noteworthy observations from the book of Genesis. First, "evil is not an eternally existing reality alongside and equal to God." Second, "evil is not *created* by this one God as an intrinsic aspect

---

a cult statue" (*The Image of God in the Garden of Eden*, Siphrut: Literature and Theology of the Hebrew Scriptures 15 [Winona Lake, IN: Eisenbrauns, 2015], 3).

of the cosmos." Instead, the evil in the world "comes from God's creatures who turn away from what is good."[35]

When preaching on evil and suffering, some key points are worth making. First, Genesis 37–50 demonstrates that God can work through unjust suffering to accomplish his good purposes. Second, the book of Judges shows how idolatry contributes to human suffering. The first narrative in the epilogue (Judges 17–21) drives home the consequences of idolatry. My big idea when I preach Judges 17–18 is: *turning from God to idols results in emptiness and bondage.*

Finally, it is also worth pointing out how easy it is to misunderstand the "retribution principle" and to assume that all personal suffering is the result of something one has done wrong.[36] Job and his friends operated this way. Job questioned God for his "unjust" suffering, and Job's friends questioned his integrity because they assumed his suffering was deserved. To be sure, the book of Job is "more about the reasons for righteousness than about the reasons for suffering."[37] But as we listen to the dialogue, we realize that Job and his friends have misapplied the retribution principle— the belief that the righteous prosper and the wicked suffer. While the retribution principle is taught in the Old Testament (see Deut. 28–30), it is a general principle, not a specific one that accounts for every ounce of human suffering.

### What Am I to Do about Evil and Suffering?

The question of what to do about evil and suffering flows from the previous one. We can help listeners respond to two kinds of evil and suffering.

First, when it comes to their own suffering, Job 28 provides a wonderful call for believers to trust in the wisdom of God. Rather than asking why the righteous suffer, we can ask why the righteous can trust God when they suffer. The answer is bound up in his wisdom and goodness.

Second, when it comes to the suffering of others, the Old Testament exhorts us again and again to practice social justice. In Isaiah 1, Yahweh indicts his people for their audacity in performing religious rituals even though they have forsaken him and have mistreated others. His plea is: "Learn to do right; seek justice. Defend the oppressed. Take up the cause of the fatherless; plead the case of the widow" (Isa. 1:17).

35. Provan, *Seriously Dangerous Religion*, 123 (emphasis original).
36. See John H. Walton and Tremper Longman III, *How to Read Job* (Downers Grove, IL: InterVarsity, 2015), 89–91.
37. Walton and Longman, *How to Read Job*, 13.

### How Am I to Relate to God?

Provan argues that love for God can rise only out of our trust in his goodness: "It is precisely because God *is* such a God that the Israelites are *commanded* to love him"[38] (see Deut. 6:4–5).

We will do well to help our listeners see the close link between obedience and love. To love God is to obey him, and to obey God is to love him (see, e.g., Deut. 11:1, 13, 22). Furthermore, we want to instill in our listeners the inestimable value of knowing God (Jer. 9:23–24) and experiencing joy in his presence (Ps. 16:11). Even an intimidating book like Leviticus is about drawing near to God. After all, one of the words for "offering" is built on a Hebrew word that means "to draw near."[39] If God's people, the Israelites, are going to draw near to a holy God, there must be atonement for sin. The animal sacrifices outlined in Leviticus taught God's people that sin costs a life. These offerings prepared the people for the arrival of Jesus, the perfect sacrifice who offered his life as a sacrifice once and for all (see Heb. 9:24–27).

### How Am I to Relate to My Neighbor?

Jesus made it clear that the entire Old Testament hangs on two commandments: to love God and to love your neighbor as yourself (Matt. 22:34–40). I suppose many listeners will be shocked to discover that God's command to love your neighbor as yourself first appears in the book of Leviticus (19:18, to be exact).

That it appears in Leviticus is telling. It reveals that neighbor love is the aim behind many of the laws in the law of Moses. The "ten words," God's basic legal policy, provide an overview of what it means to love God and neighbor. The first four commands (or words) tell God's people how to love him, while commands five through ten tell God's people how to love their neighbor. The case laws in the remainder of Exodus 20–23 and throughout the rest of the books of the Torah flesh out these basic principles in the specific circumstances in which people find themselves—farm animals falling into pits, fields destroyed by fire, lending money to people in need, and so on.

The aphorisms about how to treat one's neighbor in Proverbs and the constant calls for social justice in the prophetic books provide opportunities for preachers to help their listeners see the Old Testament's vision for loving one's neighbor.

---

38. Provan, *Seriously Dangerous Religion*, 178 (emphasis original).
39. Richard Averbeck, "*brq*" in *New International Dictionary of Old Testament Theology and Exegesis*, vol. 5, ed. Willem A. VanGemeren (Grand Rapids: Zondervan, 1997), 979.

### How Am I to Relate to the Rest of Creation?

Beginning in Genesis 1, preachers can show their listeners how the Old Testament presents God as the earth's landlord who holds his people accountable for how they treat the earth.[40] A few years ago, I preached a sermon from Genesis 1:26–28 titled "What on God's Green Earth Is a Human Being to Do?" I argued that part of our role as the image of God (see discussion above under "Who Are Man and Woman?") is to represent God by serving as caretakers of his creation.

Preachers may be afraid to tackle creation care in their preaching for fear of getting deep in the ideological weeds. Are battery-powered or hybrid cars a better means of protecting the environment than gasoline-powered ones? Or do the battery disposal issues and the potential for pollution in the energy production argue against this solution, even though battery-powered cars may run clean? We serve our listeners well when we help them evaluate ecological solutions with humility, realizing that Christians committed to creation care may disagree on how to do it.

Certainly, a passage like Deuteronomy 22:6–7 helps us reflect on how we conserve the earth's resources. This case law states: "If you come across a bird's nest beside the road, either in a tree or on the ground, and the mother is sitting on the young or on the eggs, do not take the mother with the young. You may take the young, but be sure to let the mother go, so that it may go well with you and you may have a long life." The concern seems to be preserving the source of the food supply for the future by not consuming it all in the present. We do not have to be scientists or ecologists to observe that God is calling his people to use their "renewable resources" at a reasonable rate that will sustain renewal. This principle can be applied to our use of timber, water, and minerals. I have friends in the logging industry who implement this principle by selective cutting in the forests they harvest rather than clear-cutting.

Careful preaching of the Old Testament can help the church to "bear witness to the great biblical claim that the earth is the Lord's" and "to care for the earth as an act of love and obedience to its Creator and Redeemer."[41]

### Which Society Should I Be Helping to Build?

Provan argues that "biblical faith does not advocate passivity with respect to politics, but it does not advocate, either, a utopian approach. It charts a

40. Christopher J. H. Wright, *The Mission of God: Unlocking the Bible's Grand Narrative* (Downers Grove, IL: IVP Academic, 2006), 397. Chapter 12, "Mission and God's Earth," is a fine starting point for preachers who want to expound what the Old Testament says about creation care.

41. Wright, *Mission of God*, 417–18.

middle path."[42] Our preaching will do well to emphasize how God put work in paradise rather than giving it as a punishment or allowing it to emerge as a consequence of the fall of humanity into sin.[43]

Once again, the law of Moses has something to contribute to this middle path we are trying to follow. Provan notes that "one of the purposes of biblical law . . . is simply to bring some degree of order—some degree of justice—to the world of chaos in which ancient Israel lives."[44]

A passage like Jeremiah 29:4–7 casts a vision for how God's people can live as exiles in the world. When the prophet Jeremiah wrote to the exiles in Babylon, he encouraged them to build houses, settle down, plant gardens, grow their families, and seek the peace and prosperity of the city. The vision is to contribute to human flourishing, recognizing that "my work is a critical way in which God is caring for human beings and renewing his world."[45]

### What Am I Hoping For?

The Old Testament brims with hope. Wise preachers will trace the theme of hope through the Old Testament and beyond, showing how the Bible begins and ends in a garden paradise where God is dwelling with his people—from a potential building site in Genesis 1–2 to a finished city in Revelation 21–22.[46]

This hope appears in God's promise to establish from Abraham a nation through which God would bless all peoples on earth (Gen. 12:1–3). It surfaces at various points in the Torah, such as in Deuteronomy 30:6, where God promises to perform radical heart surgery that will enable his people to love him and live. Even the endings to tragic books like Judges and Kings hint at future hope despite the fact that all hope seems lost. God's promise to establish an everlasting dynasty and kingdom through King David's offspring echoes throughout the Latter Prophets. For example, Isaiah promises a replacement of gloom with glory through the birth of a child whose reign on David's throne will never end (Isa. 9:1–7) and eventually through the new heavens and the new earth (66:22).

The point is, preachers have ample opportunity to show that the Old Testament is a book of hope. Even in the darkest texts that describe the darkest times, there is light on the horizon. Rather than Job's dire description of his

---

42. Provan, *Seriously Dangerous Religion*, 253.

43. Timothy Keller, *Every Good Endeavor: Connecting Your Work to God's Work* (New York: Riverhead Books, 2012), 23.

44. Provan, *Seriously Dangerous Religion*, 271.

45. Katherine Leary Alsdorf, foreword to Keller, *Every Good Endeavor*, xix.

46. T. Desmond Alexander, *From Eden to the New Jerusalem: An Introduction to Biblical Theology* (Grand Rapids: Kregel Academic, 2008), 14.

days that "come to an end without hope" (Job 7:6), the Old Testament constantly speaks of a hope without end (Ps. 23:6; Isa. 60:15–22).

## The Preacher's Stance and the Old Testament

The fourth world discussed by Haddon Robinson is what he calls the world of the preacher, or "your world." It is the way you (the preacher) talk, think, and handle life. Your world also includes the theological convictions you bring to the text. I refer to this as the preacher's stance. Robinson identifies two doctrines that have shaped his approach to the text over the years: human depravity and the grace of God.

Let me suggest another stance that determines how preachers study and communicate the text. This is the stance you take—or the convictions you hold—about the relationship of the Old Testament to Christ and his gospel. No one who takes the Scriptures seriously denies that the Old Testament speaks of Jesus Christ. Jesus claimed this in conversations with his followers the day he was raised from death (see Luke 24:25–27, 44–47). Yet, as Christopher Wright observes, "Preaching from the Old Testament is not just preaching *about* Jesus, though it should certainly lead people ultimately *to* Jesus."[47]

The question is how the Old Testament's anticipation of the Messiah shapes our preaching. As N. T. Wright has observed, the Old Testament is "a story in search of a conclusion."[48] This conclusion, he argues, must "incorporate the full liberation and redemption of Israel" and should correspond to and grow out of the rest of the Old Testament's story.[49] But what does this look like for preaching?

Before I address this question, I want to point out that (1) the answers to this question lie on a continuum and (2) the question itself is full of complex issues. For example, it will not work to frame the choices as "exemplary preaching" or "principle-based preaching" versus "Christ-centered preaching." Where does theocentric preaching fit? For Calvin, theocentric preaching was implicitly Christ-centered, while for Luther it was not.[50] Similarly, even

---

47. Christopher J. H. Wright, *How to Preach and Teach the Old Testament for All Its Worth* (Grand Rapids: Zondervan, 2016), 52 (emphasis original).

48. N. T. Wright, *The New Testament and the People of God* (Minneapolis: Fortress, 1992), 217. Wright says that this is how the "great story of the Hebrew scriptures" was read in the Second Temple period. Yet his observation still applies in our current world.

49. Wright, *New Testament and the People of God*, 217.

50. Sidney Greidanus, *Preaching Christ from the Old Testament: A Contemporary Hermeneutical Method* (Grand Rapids: Eerdmans, 1999), 147; see 111–51 for the full discussion of both Luther's and Calvin's approaches.

those who self-identify as "Christ-centered preachers" differ on what this approach entails.[51] Abraham Kuruvilla, who argues that "the hermeneutic of Christocentric preaching is found wanting," shrewdly labels his approach "Christiconic" since it "sees each pericope of Scripture portraying a facet of the canonical image of Christ."[52]

My modest proposal is for preachers to satisfy two legitimate concerns. One concern is to read the Old Testament in its literary and historical-cultural environment in order to determine the theological message it communicates. Such reading does not allow a Christ-centered focus to obscure "the specific thrust of individual OT texts."[53] This concern reflects my disagreement with the kind of strict Christ-centered approach that says, "We do not confront men with Christ by preaching theological ideas nor by ethical exhortations, but by rehearsing the saving events witnessed in Scripture."[54] As I have argued elsewhere, this approach is unnecessarily reductionistic. "When the apostles spoke of the gospel and rehearsed its saving events, they issued a call for nonbelievers to believe (see Acts 2:38–41 and 1 Cor. 15:1–3) and a call for believers to align their behavior with the gospel (see Gal. 2:14)."[55]

A second concern is to show how any pericope from the Old Testament and its theological message connects with the Bible's larger story line that finds its center in Christ. This is where I differ from Kuruvilla. He does not see the sermon as a place for a display of biblical theology but as "the event where the specific message of a particular text—its divine demand—is exposited and brought to bear on the life of the children of God to transform them for the glory of God."[56] But how can an Old Testament text be brought to bear on the lives of new covenant believers without noting how its theological message is shaped by its fulfillment in Christ? As William Klein, Craig Blomberg, and Robert Hubbard suggest, "We can assume neither that all of the OT carries over into the NT without any change in application nor that none of it carries over unchanged. Rather, we must examine each text to discover how it has

---

51. For example, the approaches outlined by Greidanus in *Preaching Christ*; by Bryan Chapell in *Christ-Centered Preaching: Redeeming the Expository Sermon*, 2nd ed. (Grand Rapids: Baker Academic, 2005); and by Timothy Keller in *Preaching: Communicating Faith in an Age of Skepticism* (New York: Viking, 2015) strike me as nuanced and different in some respects from each other.

52. Abraham Kuruvilla, *Privilege the Text! A Theological Hermeneutic for Preaching* (Chicago: Moody, 2013), 29.

53. Kuruvilla, *Privilege the Text!*, 239.

54. Donald G. Miller, "Biblical Theology and Preaching," *Scottish Journal of Theology* 11 (1958): 396, quoted in Greidanus, *Preaching Christ*, 235–36.

55. Mathewson, "Prophetic Preaching," 41.

56. Kuruvilla, *Privilege the Text!*, 240.

been fulfilled in Christ (Matt. 5:17)."[57] If the specifics of an Old Testament text "get swallowed up" by "biblical-theology transactions,"[58] the fault lies with the preacher—not with the methodology itself.

When I preach a narrative like 1 Samuel 17, my preaching idea is: *Yahweh wins victories through leaders who trust in his power to save.* This is the theological message of the text. When I run this story through the lens of Jesus's teaching and apostolic teaching, I do not see a need to limit or nuance its message. Granted, the victories in the New Testament are not military in nature. But we see Jesus, Paul, Peter, and others leading the advance of the gospel in hostile situations because of their trust in God's power to save.

My application of this narrative centers on abstracting from the giant that David faced to the intimidating challenges that we face when we, for example, share the gospel with Muslim neighbors or challenge a Christian friend's decision to pursue a divorce that has no biblical grounds. Whatever exhortation I offer my listeners, along with suggestions as to how they might apply this text in their lives, I ground it in the grace of God as expressed in the gospel. A sermon is sub-gospel and sub-Christian when it calls listeners to be or to do something without presenting it as a response to God's grace in the power that God's Spirit provides through the finished work of Jesus Christ.

In this particular sermon, I will typically make one more move and show how 1 Samuel 17 makes a major contribution to the developing story of the Bible. Echoing themes from the song of Hannah (1 Sam. 2:1–10), David arrives on the scene as a warrior-king who, according to Stephen Dempster, "conquers and beheads a monstrous giant, whose speech echoes the serpent's voice."[59] It is no artificial leap, then, to move in our thinking from David in 1 Samuel 17 to Jesus, the son of David, the ultimate warrior-king who defeats the beast and the kings of the earth who, like Goliath, try to set themselves up against the living God (Rev. 19:11–21). I will say all this as briefly as I have in this paragraph.

My conviction is that preachers need not pit a redemptive, Christ-centered approach against a theological, didactic approach. As D. A. Carson observed in an interview with R. C. Sproul, the New Testament writers worked with biblical-theological categories and drew moral lessons as they read the Old Testament.[60] The two are not mutually exclusive.

---

57. William W. Klein, Craig L. Blomberg, and Robert L. Hubbard Jr., *Introduction to Biblical Interpretation*, rev. ed. (Nashville: Thomas Nelson, 2004), 488–89.

58. This is Kuruvilla's concern and language in *Privilege the Text!*, 240.

59. Stephen G. Dempster, *Dominion and Dynasty: A Theology of the Hebrew Bible*, New Studies in Biblical Theology (Downers Grove, IL: InterVarsity, 2003), 140.

60. See "R. C. Sproul Interviews D. A. Carson on Biblical Exegesis," Ligonier Ministries, March 20, 2011, https://vimeo.com/20890650. The pertinent section runs from about 21:22 to

I suggest preachers ask three questions to help them move from their exegesis to the formulation of a preaching idea and its application.[61]

1. What theological message does this text communicate?
2. How does this theological message connect with the Bible's larger story line?
3. What admonition or exhortation does this story offer?

To those who fall on the side of a more theocentric approach, remember that the "prophetic message" (imperative) of an Old Testament text must always be grounded in what God has done for you in Christ (indicative). The specific emphasis of an Old Testament text must never be understood and applied apart from its connection to the meta-narrative of the Bible and the hero of that narrative: Jesus Christ.

To those who fall on the side of a more Christocentric approach, take heed of Timothy Keller's warning that "it is possible to 'get to Christ' so quickly in preaching a text that we fail to be sensitive to the particularities of the text's message. We leapfrog over historical realities to Jesus as though the Old Testament Scriptures had little significance to their original readers."[62] Remember also that Christ-centered preaching does not preclude calling the people of God to behave, as well as believe, in a certain way.

## Conclusion

Haddon Robinson believed that "Christians who don't regularly read or study the First Testament are losing part of our spiritual heritage."[63] I'm grateful for the legacy he left as a preacher who carefully studied and preached the Old Testament Scriptures. I pray that my discussion of Robinson's four worlds as they relate to the Old Testament will help preachers proclaim this part of Scripture in a way that re-reveals the living God.[64]

---

23:08. Carson's answer is in response to a question on canonical interpretation. For a lightly edited transcript of this section, see Mathewson, "Prophetic Preaching," 41–42.

61. See Mathewson, "Prophetic Preaching," 43–52.

62. Keller, *Preaching*, 60.

63. Haddon W. Robinson and Patricia Batten, *Models for Biblical Preaching: Expository Sermons from the Old Testament* (Grand Rapids: Baker Academic, 2014), vii.

64. On preaching as the "re-revelation" of God's truth, see D. A. Carson, "Challenges for the Twenty-First-Century Pulpit," in *Preach the Word: Essays on Expository Preaching; In Honor of R. Kent Hughes*, ed. Leland Ryken and Todd Wilson (Wheaton: Crossway, 2007), 176.

# 3

## The Preacher and the World of the New Testament

DUANE LITFIN

## Introduction

Haddon Robinson's lecture on the four worlds of the preacher gradually evolved over the years. Yet the version with which this book begins expresses the essential approach to preaching Haddon taught from the beginning. In this lecture he addresses the four realms the effective expositor must be prepared to navigate: the ancient world, the modern world, the specific world of the preacher's audience, and the preacher's own perceptual world. It's a classically Robinsonian take on the preaching task.

I was already fascinated by the subject of human communication when I enrolled as a student at Dallas Theological Seminary. Immediately upon hearing Haddon address these sorts of issues, I knew I had found my mentor. I quickly attached myself to him, first as his student, then as his teaching assistant. After seminary, I continued to follow his lead as I traced his academic path through my own graduate study. Eventually, at Haddon's insistence, I found myself joining the Dallas Theological Seminary faculty, teaching daily (and traveling back and forth to work) alongside my now department chair and faculty colleague. Those countless hours with Haddon, enhanced by subsequent decades of friendship and collaboration, provided me a unique education I could have gotten nowhere else. It is one I will never outgrow.

## The World of the New Testament

My task in this chapter is to focus on the first of Haddon's four worlds: the ancient world, and in particular the world of the New Testament. One might be tempted to expect in what follows a survey of the issues preachers face in dealing with that world. As Haddon argues in his lecture, a knowledge of these issues is crucial if the preacher is to do justice to the biblical text. But that knowledge will have to be gained elsewhere. The expanse of the field of New Testament studies and the limitations of the present chapter dictate that any such survey here would be so cramped and superficial as to be of little value.

Haddon specifies, for instance, the historical, linguistic, and cultural dimensions of the various worlds the preacher must negotiate. But each of these headings conceals a broad array of subtopics lurking beneath. If our goal is to understand the New Testament's *historical* background, for instance, we must ask: Which one? Jewish? Greek? Roman? Greco-Roman? If the issue is the *cultural* setting of the New Testament, which setting do we have in mind? Something broadly generic, or that of Christ's parables, or of Paul's Letter to the Galatians, or of some particular pericope in the book of Acts? Or how about the *language* of the New Testament? This involves grammar, syntax, and vocabulary, to be sure, but it also includes the literary forms and genres in which this language appears. Are we talking about the simple Greek (but deep theology) of John's Gospel, or the *Kunstprosa* of the Letter to the Hebrews? Are we seeking the latest consensus on the aorist tense, the intricacies of Greek word formation, the lexical span of some particular term?

These and a myriad of similar questions make any survey of the world of the New Testament a lengthy affair, not least because both historical developments and advances in New Testament scholarship have a way of shifting the goalposts. Who knew, for instance, that we had so much to learn about Second Temple Judaism? Or about that hybrid literary genre we call "gospel"? Or about the sociological features of the various New Testament churches? Or about the degree to which Rome's emperor cult formed the religio-political backdrop to the writings of the New Testament? Or, to zero in on a personal area of interest, what was this thing called "Greco-Roman rhetoric" and how widespread was its influence? To what extent was that Hellenistic Jew, Saul of Tarsus, trained in its persuasive strategies, and how freely did he later put these strategies to use in his letters? These sorts of contemporary debates are only a sample of what Haddon had in mind when he spoke of the need for preachers to understand the history, language, and culture of the Bible's ancient world.

I have found that even abbreviated catalogs such as the above can have an unintended effect on would-be preachers—they wind up discouraged by being reminded of all the things they do not know. Thankfully, relief is at hand in Haddon's approach to the preacher's task. The simple truth is, the typical preacher need not aspire to controlling this vast and varied body of ever-evolving information. Bible preachers are by definition generalists; they are practitioners, not (with some wonderful exceptions) scholars. Thus, setting for them the bar of the specialist's level of knowledge is a prescription for frustration and intimidation. It's a mistake Haddon always avoided.

As with most academic disciplines, there is a certain faddish quality to the field of New Testament studies. The discipline ebbs and flows as academic professionals—following in the train of the ancient Athenians, who spent their time "doing nothing but talking about and listening to the latest ideas" (Acts 17:21)—seek to stretch the boundaries of our knowledge. This is a necessary, and inevitably messy, winnowing process by which, over time, the best and most useful ideas emerge to make a lasting contribution, leaving the chaff to sail away with the wind.

Mercifully, however, the typical preacher neither can nor must keep abreast of this cutting (some would say *bleeding*) edge of the field. Up-to-date commentaries and book-length introductions or surveys serve pulpit practitioners well by providing them refined summaries of the best of the field's immense academic outpouring. If Bible preachers aspire to fulfill Haddon's call to give the historical, linguistic, and cultural background of the Scriptures their due, a manageable diet of these summative resources can serve the purpose rather well.

In any case, in lieu of a thin survey of the issues, I propose instead to address Haddon's four worlds from a different angle. I want to focus this chapter on the essential process by which effective preachers maneuver both within and between these different realms.

Successfully navigating Haddon's four worlds—that is, discerning in the ancient text (in our case, the New Testament) a faithful word from heaven and then helping a contemporary audience come to grips with what that word has to say to them—is no small challenge. When we stand to preach the Scriptures, our goal is nothing less than to deliver to our modern audience not merely our own message but a message from God, one that is fully authorized by the biblical text. Ours is thus the most precious of cargoes, which is why crossing all the necessary boundaries and time zones without sacrificing it is such a daunting assignment. My goal in this chapter is to render this challenge a little less daunting by sketching out a helpful conceptual model that clarifies what we preachers are doing—or, at least, *should* be doing—as we repeatedly attempt this perilous journey: the journey from then to now.

## The Starting Point

The task of navigating Haddon's four worlds begins with a simple but crucial insight: *The inscripturated Word of God, the Bible, is not preeminently about us; it is first and foremost a word about God.* In other words, the Bible is principally a theocentric (God-centered), not anthropocentric (human-centered), book. The purpose of this ancient compendium of writings is essentially to tell us what we need to know about our Creator: about his person, his nature, his design, his handiwork, his plan, his purposes, his will, his ways, and his actions. It is only after this—which is to say, *conceptually* after—that we can say, in a derived and secondary sense, that the Bible is also about us.

These two topics pretty much exhaust the subject matter of the Bible. Having revealed who God is and what he is doing in the world (for shorthand, let's call this dimension of biblical revelation *theology*), the Bible then calls us to respond accordingly (this dimension we'll call *application*). These two, theology and its application, constitute the essential contents of the Scriptures. Despite all its astonishing complexity and detail, in the broadest sense the entire Bible can be described in two words: *theology applied.*

This insight, simple as it is to state, has far-reaching implications for preachers. It is fundamental to understanding the biblical text and handling it well. Indeed, grasping this insight is the key to maneuvering effectively both within and between the various worlds addressed in Haddon's lecture. With regard to the ancient world, the Scriptures were composed by scores of different writers over a wide range of times and places. Yet whoever they were and whatever they were writing—law, narrative, apocalyptic, poetry, epistle, and so on—in one way or another what they were inevitably doing was bringing theological truth to bear on human life. Understanding this about what *they* were doing, in turn, informs us about what *we* are doing when we study their word and bring it to our modern world. When we attempt to exegete their various writings we do so not merely to learn about the past; we are always "mining the text," so to speak, for its relevance to the present. And that relevance—and just here lies the usefulness of our model—is to be found in the text's *theology* and *application.*

## Implicit and Explicit Ideas

Here three important observations are in order, if only to avoid misunderstanding. First, as is obvious to any student of the Bible, either or both of these dimensions of the author's message, theology or application, may in any given passage be left implicit. Whether lying on the surface or buried implicitly within, however, the very nature of the Bible is such that both theology and application are always at work in biblical texts.

Consider, for instance, the historical narratives. No story in the Bible appears there merely to report, like a newspaper account of yesterday's bank robbery, "this is what happened." The Bible's narratives do, of course, typically give us their version of "what happened." But their purpose is never merely that. As the apostle Paul reminds us, the events reported in Scripture are provided as examples "written down as warnings for us" (1 Cor. 10:6–11; cf. Rom. 15:4). The biblical writings, said Paul to Timothy, are all (*pasa graphē*) of this sort: the Scriptures are everywhere "profitable" for us precisely because they were given by God "for teaching, rebuking, correcting and training in righteousness, so that the servant of God may be thoroughly equipped for every good work" (2 Tim. 3:16–17). As a grand mosaic is comprised of its many individual pieces, so also each passage of the Bible exists to make its unique contribution to our overall understanding of who God is (theology) and what our response to him should be (application).

Second, it is also important to stress that we discover this applied theology not by leapfrogging the details of the text but precisely by giving them their due. Whatever theology or application the biblical author is communicating will inevitably be communicated *through* these details. All such features of the text require our fullest attention—treating poetry as poetry, parable as parable, epistle as epistle, apocalyptic as apocalyptic, and so on. But we will leave these details short if we fail to work ourselves all the way through to their ultimate import: namely, what they contribute to our understanding of God and what this means in turn for how we are to respond. The exegetical dexterity required to accomplish this goal aright, across the various literary genres of the Bible, is not easy or quick to come by. But it is a dexterity preachers must master if they are to handle the Scriptures well.

Third, so also it is with our preaching. The biblical authors were not the only ones called to bring an authoritative word from God to their listeners. In its own way this is also the task of biblical preaching. When we open the Scriptures before a modern audience, ours too is an exercise in the application of theology to life. Our task is to help our listeners discover what the biblical author is telling us about God and how this truth is relevant to us today. "This is what God is revealing about himself in this passage," we keep saying, in essence, "and this is the difference he wills this truth to make in our lives." In this way the biblical text and the message preached can both be summarized as *theology applied*.

I recognize, of course, that I am painting here, so far, high off the ground and with a very broad brush. This inevitably raises a flurry of practical questions. Years of teaching on this subject, often in a classroom alongside Haddon Robinson, assure me that with sufficient time for clarification and nuance, these questions melt away. But our present venue allows neither the time nor space for such exploration. So I will settle instead for drawing at least the outline of a model that demonstrates the core *theology applied* premise at work. Little about this model is original with me, but I have found the following way of describing it uniquely helpful.

## The Model's Scaffolding[1]

The scaffolding for our model is the iconic "ladder of abstraction," long associated with the general semantics movement founded by the Polish-born scholar Alfred Korzybski. Korzybski was fascinated by the way humans think and use language. He focused in particular on the process of abstraction.[2] His later followers, most notably California university professor (and later US senator) S. I. Hayakawa, popularized what came to be known as the ladder of abstraction.[3]

Abstraction is, so to speak, the process of leaving out detail.[4] As we move up the ladder from below, our terms become less specific. For example, "Fido" names a category of one; he is a particular brown and white cocker spaniel. But as we move up to the category "dog," all of Fido's unique characteristics are left behind as we focus only on those features he shares with other dogs. At the next higher level of abstraction, "mammal," even Fido's "dog-ness" is left behind as we focus on only those features he shares with other mammals (as against, say, fish or trees). And so on, all the way up the ladder of

1. This section is adapted from Duane Litfin, *Word versus Deed: Resetting the Scales to a Biblical Balance* (Wheaton: Crossway, 2012), 64–67.

2. See Alfred Korzybski, *Science and Sanity: An Introduction to Non-Aristotelian Systems and General Semantics* (Brooklyn: Institute of General Semantics, 1933), chap. 25.

3. S. I. Hayakawa, *Language and Thought in Action* (New York: Harcourt Brace & World, 1964), 177–79.

4. In technical philosophical terms, abstractions are high-order super-collective nouns. Rather than limiting ourselves to this technical definition, however, in what follows I will use the ladder of abstraction more loosely to refer not only to abstractions proper but also to such things as general ideas and their particular implications, or large theological affirmations and their specific applications or entailments.

abstraction. The higher we go, the broader, less detailed, and more inclusive our terms become; the lower we move, the more concrete and specific. That's why we can say the process of abstracting (moving up the ladder) is the process of leaving out detail. Korzybski wanted us to understand this process so that we could appreciate both the wonders and the pitfalls of abstractions.

There are some who seem to delight in disparaging "mere abstractions," as if we could live without them. But this is a foolish mistake. The ability to abstract is the genius of the human mind. Alligators or mosquitoes or dogs cannot think of abstractions such as "mammals," or "love," or "justice," much less an equation such as $E = mc^2$. They experience the concrete particulars of the world, but they cannot reflect upon those details and analyze them. Only humans can create the required abstractions and then put them to use.

"Great thoughts are always general," said Samuel Johnson in his *Lives of the English Poets*.[5] And so they are. Every wise proverb is useful precisely because it represents a powerful abstraction, often in humble dress. Jesus's language was full of the highest order metaphors (e.g., "I am the way and the truth and the life" [John 14:6]), each one embodying a powerful abstraction. The greatest human minds throughout history have been those marked by their ability to think at levels of abstraction that leave most of us behind. Thus it makes no sense to valorize the concrete at the expense of the abstract. To do so is to "induce upon ourselves" what C. S. Lewis called a "doglike mind": "You will have noticed that most dogs cannot understand *pointing*. You point to a bit of food on the floor; the dog, instead of looking at the floor, sniffs at your finger. A finger is a finger to him, and that is all. His world is all fact and no meaning."[6]

A contempt for abstractions consigns us to this doglike mind wherein everything is experienced as an animal experiences it. Such contempt is misguided. Not only is it a denial of something wonderfully and uniquely human; we could not live without abstractions if we wished to. Those who complain about abstractions use abstractions (such as the term "abstractions") to do so. Abstractions are a form of shorthand we cannot do without. They help us manage the complexity of the world around us. They are what make the best of human thought and conversation possible. They are indispensable.

What we should avoid, on the other hand—and what, I suspect, most critics really have in mind when they disparage abstractions as such—is what Wendell Johnson called "dead-level abstracting."[7] Hayakawa described this

5. Samuel Johnson, *Lives of the English Poets*, in *The Works of Samuel Johnson* (New York: Alexander V. Blake, 1846), 2:8.
6. C. S. Lewis, "Transposition," in *The Weight of Glory*, ed. Walter Hooper (New York: Collier, 1980), 71.
7. Wendell Johnson, *People in Quandaries* (New York: Harper, 1946), 270.

common problem this way: "Some people, it appears, remain more or less permanently stuck at certain levels of the abstraction ladder, some on the lower levels, some on the very high levels."[8] Such "dead-level" conversations on the lower rungs of the ladder can be tiresome and boring. But others seem equally locked in at the upper levels. Everything remains in the realm of the general, never descending to the particular—what Wendell Johnson calls "words cut loose from their moorings."[9] We have all heard preachers and teachers who fall into this trap, and we have all read dull, obtuse books in which scarcely a concrete statement can be found. This tendency too is to be avoided.

The ability and willingness to move up and down the abstraction ladder is the mark not only of interesting communicators but of clear and sound thinkers as well. The field of general semantics was developed as a way to encourage this kind of "good mental hygiene." Effective thinkers/communicators are constantly reflecting on the particulars in such a way as to build useful generalizations and then testing those generalizations against the particulars. They move up and down the ladder of abstraction, allowing the general to inform and give meaning to the particulars, while allowing the particulars to flesh out and anchor the general. Scientists, for example, build broad hypotheses on the basis of their observations of the details and then design experiments with the details to test their broad hypotheses. Great literature is timeless precisely because it conveys large ideas through the telling of concrete stories. (As someone has said, "Newspapers tell us what *happened*; literature tells us what *happens*.") Great orators and essayists range up and down the ladder in their works, allowing the abstract to provide meaning and context to the particulars, and the particulars to flesh out and bring to life the abstract. Effective preachers and politicians do the same. Says Hayakawa, "The interesting writer, the informative speaker, [and] the accurate thinker . . . operate on all levels of the abstraction ladder, moving quickly and gracefully and in orderly fashion from the higher to the lower, from lower to higher, with minds as lithe and deft and beautiful as monkeys in a tree."[10]

## The Model Applied

This is the pattern at work in the Bible. All of the Bible can be arrayed, so to speak, up and down the ladder of abstraction. The substance of the Bible's message is theocentric truth (by definition general; i.e., true for all) applied

8. Hayakawa, *Language and Thought in Action*, 188.
9. Johnson, *People in Quandaries*, 273.
10. Hayakawa, *Language and Thought in Action*, 166.

to particular lives (specific). Not every passage in the Bible *explicitly* exhibits this range, of course, but some such range is implicit everywhere. The Bible is constantly, either explicitly or implicitly, moving up and down the abstraction ladder.

None of this should surprise us. God designed us to live on this ladder. We are embodied persons making our way in the physical and social world God has made; all of us experience a variety of concrete needs and situations. But we are also thinking, feeling, spiritual creatures. We are made in God's image and share aspects of his own nature. Unlike the lesser creatures, we crave the meaning, significance, and purpose that only the larger truths can provide. We live our lives all up and down the abstraction ladder, from top to bottom.

Some books of the Bible reflect this reality structurally. For instance, the six chapters of Ephesians divide elegantly into two halves. The first three explore in broad strokes what God is doing in the world through Christ. Such ideas are necessarily high and large and inclusive. God's purpose, Paul says, was "to make plain to everyone the administration of this mystery, which for ages past was kept hidden in God, who created all things. His intent was that now, through the church, the manifold wisdom of God should be made known to the rulers and authorities in the heavenly realms, according to his eternal purpose that he accomplished in Christ Jesus our Lord" (Eph. 3:9–11).

The next three chapters, however, deal with the equally concrete details of life. They include such specific instructions as these: "Among you there must not be even a hint of sexual immorality, or of any kind of impurity, or of greed, because these are improper for God's holy people. Nor should there be obscenity, foolish talk or coarse joking, which are out of place, but rather thanksgiving" (Eph. 5:3–4).

How are the two halves of Ephesians, the general and the specific, related? The bridge is found in 4:1: "I urge you to live a life worthy of the calling you have received." The abstract truths of chapters 1–3 spell out the "calling" of the church, a calling that bears concrete implications for how God's people are to live. Our behavior receives its shape and meaning from the abstract truths of which it is an expression. Neither can stand alone: *truth-informed behavior* and *behavior-enacted truth* are two sides of the same coin.

The large ideas of God's Word, then, always bear implications for how we are to live. Sometimes those ideas are focused on *who God is*: "Whoever does not love does not know God, because God is love" (1 John 4:8). At other times they tell us *what God is like*: Jesus's parable of the unjust judge shows us that God is such that his people "should always pray and not give up" (Luke 18:1). Other ideas focus on *what God has done*: "Therefore, brothers and sisters, since we have confidence to enter the Most Holy Place by the blood of Jesus, by the new and living way opened for us through the curtain, that is, his body, and since we have a great priest over the house of God, let us . . . Let us . . . And let us . . ." (Heb. 10:19–25). Still other ideas tell us *what God will yet do*: "But the day of the Lord will come like a thief. The heavens will disappear with a roar; the elements will be destroyed by fire, and the earth and everything done in it will be laid bare. Since everything will be destroyed in this way, what kind of people ought you to be? You ought to live holy and godly lives" (2 Pet. 3:10–11). And so on. One way or another, God's truth always bears implications for our living. Hence Paul's prayer (Col. 1:9–10) that his readers might be filled "with the knowledge of his will through all the wisdom and understanding that the Spirit gives" (theology). Why? "So that you may live a life worthy of the Lord and please him in every way: bearing fruit in every good work" (application). Just so: *theology*, *applied*.

So strong is the connection between the general and the specific in the Christian life that defaulting on either may call into question the whole. The all-encompassing abstract affirmation "Jesus is Lord," for example, is the very hallmark of the believer. No one can sincerely affirm it, says Paul, except by the Holy Spirit (1 Cor. 12:3). In fact, the failure to affirm it is the surest sign of a lack of genuineness (2 John 1:7–11), whatever our behavior. But the opposite is also true. The book of James famously connects the abstract with the concrete in its discussion of faith and works: "What good is it, my brothers and sisters, if someone claims to have faith but has no deeds? Can such faith save them?" (2:14).

What does James mean here by "such faith," the kind that cannot save? It is the faith, he says, of the demons: "You believe that there is one God. Good! Even the demons believe that—and shudder" (2:19). The faith that cannot save is a faith that perches high up the ladder of abstraction and never comes down. It consists of little more than mental assent to Israel's ancient Shema: "The LORD our God, the LORD is one" (Deut. 6:4). But this monotheistic acknowledgment, understood all too well in the demonic realm, is not a faith that saves. The faith that saves takes in the next verse as well: "Love the LORD your God with all your heart and with all your soul and with all your strength" (6:5). While genuine saving faith certainly includes elements of mental assent, it also involves more: it involves personally entrusting ourselves to the one God and then living according to his Word—something the demons will never do.

Note that this kind of faith, the kind that saves, does not disdain or repudiate the abstract. On the contrary, it stands in full agreement with the great abstract affirmation of the Shema: "God is one." Genuine faith in fact hungers for *more* abstract knowledge about God. Who is he? What are his attributes? What is he like? What are his ways? The difference is that saving faith does not *settle* for the abstract. It wants to know not only "about" God; it seeks to know him personally and to serve him faithfully. It wants to honor him and worship him and fellowship with him. It seeks to understand his will and obey it. It aspires "to live a life worthy of his calling" in every way. This is what distinguishes biblical faith from mere mental assent. Real faith is lived up and down the ladder of abstraction. Anything short of this, the Bible warns, may not be genuine faith at all.

## Using the Model

Because the Bible is essentially about applying theology to life, the *theology applied* model becomes a useful way of conceptualizing what we are doing as we maneuver both within and between Haddon's four worlds. Two familiar New Testament passages illustrate the point well.

The first passage is Paul's classic reference to "oxen" in his appeal to the Corinthians:

> Who serves as a soldier at his own expense? Who plants a vineyard and does not eat its grapes? Who tends a flock and does not drink the milk? Do I say this merely on human authority? Doesn't the Law say the same thing? For it is written in the Law of Moses: "Do not muzzle an ox while it is treading out the grain." Is it about oxen that God is concerned? Surely he says this for us, doesn't he? Yes, this was written for us, because whoever plows and threshes should be able to do so in the hope of sharing in the harvest. If we have sown spiritual seed among you, is it too much if we reap a material harvest from you? (1 Cor. 9:7–11)

This passage nicely illustrates the points we have been making. For starters, it is thoroughly theocentric. Despite its abundance of concrete references, it is first and foremost about discerning God's essential concern: "Is it about oxen that God is concerned? Surely he says this for us, doesn't he?" Paul's priority was that his readers understand the heart and intent of God. All the specific applications, from oxen to apostles, flow from that.

This passage also illustrates the *theology applied* nature of the biblical text. Within these few verses we can see the apostle moving up and down the ladder of abstraction. The concrete application to oxen in Deuteronomy 25 was the outworking, Paul insists, of a broader, more general truth that applied to not only work animals but also soldiers, vine dressers, shepherds, plowmen, threshers, and Christian workers. It is essentially the same premise Jesus applied to his disciples when he sent them out two by two: "The worker deserves his wages" (Luke 10:7). This abstract principle expresses an important element of justice in God's design and intent for his entire creation. It is this broader theocentric insight, Paul says, that is at work in the law's concrete reference to oxen, on the one hand, and his own situation in Corinth, on the other. From the law's treatment of oxen, up to the broader theocentric truth that informs that treatment, and back down to his circumstances in Corinth, Paul's argument is arrayed up and down the ladder of abstraction.

## Both Directions

Like Paul, exegetes and expositors must be ready to work in both directions on this ladder. Sometimes we are required to think our way up the ladder, as when moving from the specifics regarding oxen to the theocentric justice principle that informs those specifics. At other times, the opposite is true. The high-order truths in the Bible entail implications that are to be worked out in the details of our lives.

For a classic example of this move down the ladder, consider a second passage. The universal testimony of the Bible is that God is "holy." But Scripture also teaches that this general truth about God bears specific implications for those who claim to be his people. Peter made this connection explicit when he wrote to his readers, "But just as he who called you is holy, so be holy in all you do; for it is written, 'Be holy, because I am holy'" (1 Pet. 1:15–16). Peter's citation is drawn from Leviticus 11:44: "I am the Lord your God; consecrate yourselves and be holy, because I am holy."

These dual references to holiness provide an especially clear example of the *theology-application* relationship in biblical passages. What is true about God bears implications for what is to be true about his people. The broad *truth* that "God is holy" entails the requirement that those who belong to and represent him are to be "holy" as well. Similarly, the broad *promises* found in the Bible (e.g., "Never will I leave you; never will I forsake you") are to be trusted and acted upon in the specifics of daily life ("Keep your lives free from the love of money and be content with what you have" [Heb. 13:5]). Or again, God's general *instructions* (e.g., "Love your neighbor as yourself" [Mark 12:31]) are to be lived out with regard to actual people ("A man was going down from Jerusalem to Jericho . . ." [Luke 10:30]). All of the Bible is arrayed up and down the ladder of abstraction, from the general to the specific and back again.

Finally, observe how these two examples (the treatment of oxen and the holiness of God) illustrate the move preachers must make not only within the ancient worlds but also between them. In each case the theocentric element is determinative; all else flows from that. It is the theology—what is true of God—that provides the primary link between then and now.

God is holy, says the Bible, and he calls those who know him as their God to emulate him. This is a theocentric truth about the nature and will of God that is as true and weighty for us as it was for both ancient Israel and, much later, Peter and his generation. This theological truth is transtemporal and transcultural precisely because it is a truth about God. Its relevance thus spans the generations.

On the other hand, as we move down the ladder, the application of that truth may vary as the audience's situation changes—and the more disparate those situations, the more disparate the applications may become. We see this variation already between Leviticus 11 and 1 Peter 1. For the ancient Israelites, the move down the ladder to specific application meant (among many other things) obeying the Levitical food laws: "consecrate yourselves and be holy, because I am holy. Do not make yourselves unclean by any creature that moves along the ground. I am the LORD, who brought you up out of Egypt to be your God; therefore be holy, because I am holy" (Lev. 11:44–45). Many generations later, when Peter moved down the ladder to his audience from exactly the same theocentric premise, the application sounded like this: "As obedient children, do not conform to the evil desires you had when you lived in ignorance. But just as he who called you is holy, so be holy in all you do" (1 Pet. 1:14–15).

It is not difficult to demonstrate that, unlike the ancient Israelites, "holiness" for Peter's audience did not entail following the Levitical food laws. As Peter himself learned the hard way (Acts 10:9–16), this application was, for theological reasons, no longer appropriate. So despite a common theocentric premise, the applicatory dimensions of Leviticus 14 and 1 Peter 1 differ dramatically. What happens, then, when we add in still a third audience, a contemporary one? The theocentric premise changes not at all. It is only as we move down the ladder toward application, as did Peter, that the application may change.

A contemporary Christian audience shares with Peter's audience the same theological dissimilarity to the ancient Israelites; by God's design, neither Christian audience is bound by the Levitical food laws. Thus Peter's move down the ladder, cited above, is as relevant to our audience as it was to his own. But notice that this is because Peter's application ("Be holy in all you do") is still general enough—which is to say, high enough on the ladder—to subsume both his and a contemporary audience. As we move further down the ladder to greater specificity, however, the cultural and chronological

differences between these two Christian audiences begin to generate diver-
gence. It is unlikely, for example, that the use of pornography would show
up on any first-century list of the kinds of things Peter had in mind when he
spoke of "the passions of your former ignorance." In our day, however, this
might well be a pertinent (and needful) application of what it means to be
holy as God is holy.

## Some Concluding Observations

1. It is important never to lose sight of our working premise: *The Scriptures
   are not preeminently about us; they are first and foremost about God.*
   The Bible is essentially a *theocentric* book. Keeping this in mind will
   help us avoid common anthropocentric distortions of the biblical text,
   such as (to use a real-world example) construing Jesus's affirmation in
   John 3:16 of God's extraordinary love for the world as evidence of how
   lovable the world must be (*anthropocentric*) instead of how loving God
   is (*theocentric*). When we trade the anthropocentric for the theocentric,
   it's as if we are examining the Bible through the wrong end of a telescope.
   It's no wonder what we see is distorted.

2. As Haddon often said (and wrote), "Thinking is hard work, and thinking about thinking is even harder work." The *theology applied* model
   highlights this aspect of the preacher's calling. Biblical preachers are
   inherently required to think deeply about the thinking of the biblical
   author; then they must think deeply about how this truth applies to
   their contemporary audience. This process requires rigorous mental
   effort even in the most straightforward of passages. It becomes even
   more demanding when elements of the biblical author's thought are
   left implicit. The ever-present danger is that as we move up and down
   our theoretical ladder, bringing to the surface the passage's implicit
   theology and attempting to apply it to our audience, we will subtly and
   inadvertently find ourselves having shifted to a related but different ladder.[11] This exegetical mistake is too complex to explore here, but suffice

---

11. Preachers should always attempt to bring what is implicit in the passage to conscious
expression for the sake of their own *exegetical reflection* on the author's ideas. But it need not
follow that what is implicit in the text must always become explicit *in the message itself.* That
implicit material should drive the sermon in the same way it implicitly drives the passage, but there
are occasions—for instance, think of one of Haddon Robinson's first-person narratives—where,
just as in the passage itself, what is communicated to the preacher's audience is communicated
via "indirection." This sort of implicit communication is difficult to do, much less to do well,
but in principle it remains one of the preacher's options.

it to say, allowing this to happen is a prescription for misunderstanding and misrepresenting the biblical text rather than expositing it.

3. The *theology applied* model highlights the preacher's need to understand the ancient worlds of the Bible. In Romans 14, for instance, Paul's teaching regarding the weaker brother is a classic example of *theology applied*. But we will not likely do justice to this teaching if we do not understand the application issues (eating, drinking, special days) that were at stake for those ancient believers. This in turn will hinder our ability to discern the theology that is driving these applications. The ability to trace the apostle's moves up and down the ladder, tracking his argument from theology to application and back again, is critical to understanding how to apply the passage in our own setting.

4. Due to the overall theocentric focus of the Scriptures, the *theology applied* model suggests that (to use Haddon's standard terms) the *exegetical idea* of the text will typically be couched at the theological level, or in terms of that theology and its application. In the same way, as we bridge to our audience, we do well to try to reflect this same pattern in our *homiletical idea*. This will tend to keep our preaching theocentric. In an age of widespread anthropocentric preaching, the *theology applied* model enables us to show up again and again with a potent word from God about God. It is a timeless word that transcends us all because it speaks of a timeless God who transcends us all. But as it was for the biblical author, so also for us: it is a timeless word with always timely implications for who we are, who we are to become, and how we are to live. Space limitations preclude exploring this complex issue here, but for help on how all of this works together, see Haddon's *Biblical Preaching*.[12]

5. We have primarily been addressing Haddon's first three worlds—that is, moving exegetically within the ancient text and its worlds, and then bridging hermeneutically to bring God's Word to bear on the modern worlds of our listeners. Here I want to finish with a brief nod to Haddon's fourth world, that of the preacher. The more we preachers understand about our own limitations and truncated perspectives, the more fearful it becomes to stand before an audience and proclaim, "Thus saith the Lord." Yet it is to precisely this that the expository preacher is called. Our proclamation must be done humbly, recognizing the frailties inherent in both our understanding of the text and our attempts to bring

12. Haddon W. Robinson, *Biblical Preaching: The Development and Delivery of Expository Messages*, 3rd ed. (Grand Rapids: Baker Academic, 2014).

its theocentric truth down the ladder to bear upon the concrete details of life for our listeners. Yet if we have been called by God to proclaim his Word, we can do no other. As the apostle Paul put it, "We have this treasure in jars of clay to show that this all-surpassing power is from God and not from us" (2 Cor. 4:7). The business of the Bible—*theology applied*—is by definition also the business of the Bible preacher.

# 4

## The Preacher's Personal World

SCOTT M. GIBSON

### Introduction

The preacher's personal world is not always discernible to listeners when they hear the preacher preach from week to week. We are, as the psalmist describes, "fearfully and wonderfully made" (Ps. 139:14), and yet we are equally not without sin, "not even one" (Rom. 3:10). If we are honest with ourselves, we would admit that what takes place on the inside has the potential—for good or ill—to drive that which is on the outside in our lives, having an impact on the ministry God has given us. What is happening inside of us is seen in what we do and say.

Jesus images this principle when he warns his listeners: "No good tree bears bad fruit, nor does a bad tree bear good fruit. Each tree is recognized by its own fruit." The true inner reality is seen—or at least a partial view of it is revealed. Jesus continues, "A good man brings good things out of the good stored up in his heart, and an evil man brings evil things out of the evil stored up in his heart." Jesus then clarifies the image by stating the idea he is getting at: "For the mouth speaks what the heart is full of" (Luke 6:43–45).

This chapter is about the heart, the inner world of the preacher, the preacher's personal world, what we store, cultivate, consider, cling to, desire, imagine, cloak, hide, treasure, honor, value, and all the rest of what is beneath the surface of our lives that has an impact on our relationship with the Lord, ourselves, our spouse (if we are married), the congregations we serve, and what we are to do to develop our personal world. We are talking about character. Os Guinness reflects: "Thus character is clearly distinct from such concepts as personality, image, reputation, or celebrity. Applied to a person, it is the essential 'stuff' he or she is made of, the inner reality in which thoughts, speech, decisions, behavior, and relations are rooted. As such, character determines behavior just as behavior demonstrates character."[1]

The inner world of the preacher is where one cultivates the characteristics of Christian maturity—one's character. There are various dimensions to one's character, some developed or underdeveloped; some parts are continuing to mature, while other aspects are less mature and are more of a challenge to change.

What makes a mature preacher—one who is able to lead a congregation, to preach with the confidence that comes from a consistent life that reflects the values and the truths he or she preaches? We begin with the essence of character as suggested above.

## Character Means Maturing in Christ

Paul's purpose statement in Colossians 1:28–29 is for every preacher: Christ "is the one we proclaim, admonishing and teaching everyone with all wisdom, so that we may present everyone fully mature in Christ. To this end I strenuously contend with all the energy Christ so powerfully works in me." Paul's goal—to make everyone perfect in Christ—highlights the intended trajectory of every follower of Jesus Christ, including those who are called to preach and lead God's people.

The word Paul uses for "perfect" (*teleion*) can also be translated "mature, grown-up."[2] A Christian is expected to grow in the faith in order to reflect the Savior, Jesus Christ. As a pastor, Paul took seriously his responsibility to be moving Christians to maturity.

The etymological meaning of the word "character" is "an indelible mark, an etching, inscribing, engraving, or imprinting." This force—often external— "changes the shape, orientation, and manifestation of one's self."[3] Character formation for our purposes is not based on Aristotle's understanding of virtue or character. His was an emphasis on the external or "perceived" character

---

1. Os Guinness, *When No One Sees: The Importance of Character in an Age of Image* (Colorado Springs: NavPress, 2000), 15–16.

2. See, e.g., Curtis Vaughan, "Colossians," in *The Expositor's Bible Commentary*, ed. Frank E. Gaebelein (Grand Rapids: Zondervan, 1978), 193.

3. Andre Resner, "Character," in *The New Interpreter's Handbook of Preaching*, ed. Paul Scott Wilson (Nashville: Abingdon, 2008), 225.

and its influence particularly in rhetoric.[4] For him the "virtuous person always tended to be that of the 'hero,' the moral giant striding through the world doing great deeds and gaining applause."[5] Although Aristotle, Seneca, and other pagan moralists told people how to live, they were unable to live well themselves.[6]

For Christians, what distinguishes the development of character from Greek or Hebrew understandings is that one's character is shaped by biblical revelation and by the work of the Holy Spirit. Character formation takes place in the crucible of the church, where mature men and women of faith pour their lives into infant believers born again into the family of faith, moving them to maturity in Christ.

Character development, then, begins in Christian discipleship in the local church, in relationships of care with the purpose of shaping men and women and girls and boys into Christlikeness. Francis Greenwood Peabody recognized this discipleship pattern of character development, rooted in the local church. Peabody stated:

> If the Christian religion were primarily doctrinal, it might have been taught by a book instead of a person, and have offered a system instead of a saviour; if it were primarily emotional, it might have been taught by nature or experience, in wonder or fear, in joy or pain, by miracle or sign. A religion which begins in righteousness and is fulfilled in love must, on the other hand, be communicated by a person to a person. Will is moved by will. Character answers to character.[7]

The preacher cannot ignore the importance of growth in maturity in Christ. When one stands to preach, one's character is reflected, revealed. That is what preaching is and does. Bryan Chapell urges: "True character cannot be hidden, although it can be temporarily masked. Character oozes out of us in our messages. Just as people reveal themselves in conversations by their words and mannerisms, we constantly reveal ourselves to others in our preaching. Over time our word choices, topics, examples, and tone unveil our hearts regardless of how well we think we have cordoned off deeper truths from public display."[8]

---

4. Resner, "Character," 226.

5. N. T. Wright, *After You Believe: Why Christian Character Matters* (New York: Harper-Collins, 2010), 70.

6. See Aristotle, *The Nicomachean Ethics*, trans. J. E. C. Welldon (Buffalo: Prometheus, 1987). See also Wright, *After You Believe*, 138.

7. Francis Greenwood Peabody, *Jesus Christ and the Christian Character* (New York: Macmillan, 1905), 126–27.

8. Bryan Chapell, *Christ-Centered Preaching: Redeeming the Expository Sermon*, 2nd ed. (Grand Rapids: Baker Academic, 2005), 37.

The person called to preach must be anchored in the life of the local church, where one's call is confirmed and one's life is shaped by the community of faith. There are cases in which this dimension is absent from a preacher's biography. Sometimes a person is converted to Christ through a campus ministry while studying at university. Through the campus fellowship, a network of relationships nurtures the believer, shaping him or her into the image of Christ. Some sense a call to ministry, and they go to seminary after college. The believer may attend a local church while in college, but the main teaching and spiritual development comes primarily from the campus ministry. The experience of the local church is somewhat foreign to the new believer, yet he or she wants to become a pastor. For someone who is converted while in college through a campus ministry, the best next step is to join a local church while in seminary to gain experience and nurture from a community of mature believers. William P. Brown acknowledges, "The development of the self is consistently framed in relation to other selves: God, parent, friend, or foe, flat or full. Character in the end of itself is necessarily character in *relation*."[9] That is where the local church comes in—to shape the lives of those who are a part of it.

Intentional inner development and inter-development of the preacher's character is what will shape the preacher's world and the way in which that world is understood and perceived by those in the church and outside the church. But how does the preacher develop character? The next section provides insight regarding this question.

## Growing in Christ

The preacher is to nurture a personal relationship with the Lord, which is foundational for preaching. How we tend to our inner personal world and how we take care of our personal world that interacts with others—our inter-development—affects our maturity, our character. As Dave McClellan reminds us, "The implication here is that the preacher needs to have an identity before God and people that is deeper than the preaching role. We need to become lovers of God first. Lovers of people second."[10] Growth in Christ involves intentional inner development and intentional inter-development. We will explore what this means next.

9. William P. Brown, *Character in Crisis: A Fresh Approach to the Wisdom Literature of the Old Testament* (Grand Rapids: Eerdmans, 1996), 151.
10. Dave McClellan, *Preaching by Ear: Speaking God's Truth from the Inside Out* (Wooster, OH: Weaver, 2014), 45.

### *Intentional Inner Development*

Diligent personal commitment to Christ is key for pastoral integrity and character. A clearly defined relationship with the Savior will provide stability. Paul warned the Corinthian believers, "So, if you think you are standing firm, be careful that you don't fall!" (1 Cor. 10:12). Taking our spiritual temperature gives us perspective and urges us to take care of that which displeases the Lord, and it prompts us to continue to cultivate the attitudes and practices in our lives that honor the Lord. Our relationship with Christ is strengthened when we practice the following: confession, repentance, holiness, prayer, and Bible reading. These are keys to intentional inner development.

## CONFESSION OF SIN KNOWN AND UNKNOWN

Confession of our sins to the Lord enables us to recognize our place before the sovereign Lord of the universe and to receive forgiveness from him. He is God, and we are not. We want to be aware of our sinful state, but we also desire to celebrate the hope of the gospel, which is the forgiveness of sin. Because of forgiveness, we want to, as Jerry Bridges encourages, preach the gospel "to ourselves every day," which will enable us to appreciate and live in forgiveness.[11] There are two kinds of confession. The first is the confession we make at the initial submission of our sinful selves to the Savior in salvation. Yet confession is not a one-time undertaking. Confession for the believer continues throughout one's life, which is the second form of confession of sin. John reminds us, "If we confess our sins, he is faithful and just and will forgive us our sins and purify us from all unrighteousness" (1 John 1:9). Because of what Jesus Christ did for us on the cross and his vindication in victory over death, both the sins that we know and confess and the sins that we do not know we have committed are forgiven. In the prayers for confession of sin, the Book of Common Prayer puts it this way:

> Most merciful God,
> we confess that we have sinned against thee
> in thought, word, and deed,
> by what we have done,
> and by what we have left undone.
> We have not loved thee with our whole heart;
> we have not loved our neighbors as ourselves.
> We are truly sorry and we humbly repent.

11. Jerry Bridges, *The Discipline of Grace: God's Role and Our Role in the Pursuit of Holiness* (Colorado Springs: NavPress, 1994), 46. See the entire chap. 3, pp. 45–60.

For the sake of thy Son Jesus Christ,
have mercy on us and forgive us;
that we may delight in thy will,
and walk in thy ways,
to the glory of thy Name. Amen.[12]

We want to be preachers who acknowledge our need for a savior, for constant forgiveness, and for total dependence on our Lord as we live life and preach God's Word. We practice this by confessing our sins.

What does this look like in daily life? The prayer the Lord taught his disciples is a reminder to Pastor Karen (a real person but not her real name) that confession of sin did not stop at her conversion to Christ. The Lord's Prayer is a prayer Pastor Karen prays every day. "Forgive us our sins, for we also forgive everyone who sins against us," Jesus instructs as he teaches his first-century disciples—and us—how to pray (Luke 11:4; cf. Matt. 6:12). "Confession clears the way for an open, vibrant relationship with the Lord," notes Karen. For her—and for us—confession is a constant and necessary practice.

### Repentance from Sin, a Repentance That Is Ongoing

Not only do we confess our sins but, as the prayer above indicates—"We are truly sorry and we humbly repent"—we turn away from the practice of committing again the sin we confessed. Repentance means to turn 180 degrees away from the sin that we just confessed.

There are two distinct types of repentance. The first is when we initially come in faith to Jesus Christ as Savior and receive eternal life. Because of God's grace—his kindness to us in Christ—we move from death because of our sins to life because of Christ. The Ephesian believers were reminded of their initial repentance when Paul emphasized to them:

As for you, you were dead in your transgressions and sins, in which you used to live when you followed the ways of this world and of the ruler of the kingdom of the air, the spirit who is now at work in those who are disobedient. All of us also lived among them at one time, gratifying the cravings of our flesh and following its desires and thoughts. Like the rest, we were by nature deserving of wrath. But because of his great love for us, God, who is rich in mercy, made us alive with Christ even when we were dead in transgressions—it is by grace you have been saved. And God raised us up with Christ and seated us with him in the heavenly realms in Christ Jesus, in order that in the coming ages he

12. *The Book of Common Prayer and Administration of the Sacraments and Other Rites and Ceremonies of the Church* (New York: Seabury, 1979), 116–17.

might show the incomparable riches of his grace, expressed in his kindness to us in Christ Jesus. For it is by grace you have been saved, through faith—and this is not from yourselves, it is the gift of God—not by works, so that no one can boast. (Eph. 2:1–9)

Pastor Simon came to faith in Christ when he was in high school. He was not raised in a Christian home and knew little about what it meant to be a Christian. Simon worked at a fruit and vegetable stand with other high school students. Their lives were different. Simon could see the difference as they interacted with each other and the customers. Finally, one of the high school girls invited Simon to a Christian music concert that was held at a little country Baptist church. He agreed to go. Prompted by the music and the pastor's brief explanation of the gospel at the end of the concert, Simon confessed his sin and his need for Christ's forgiveness, repented from his life of faithlessness, and became a follower of Christ. This was his initial confession of sin that came in response to the hope of gospel forgiveness. He says that he daily confesses and repents—throughout the day and in his daily time of prayer with the Lord. "I need a clear, open relationship with the Lord," he underscores, which is another kind of repentance.

The repentance that is repeated throughout a believer's life is a second type of repentance. When we commit a specific sin and are confronted by it, we confess it—and we repent from committing that sin again. The Corinthian Christians were challenged by their pastor, Paul, in his letter to them about various sins evident in their life as a church. They responded to his words by repenting, turning from their sins. The conviction and confrontation that came from the letter was not easy for them to receive, and Paul knew this. He reflects, "Even if I caused you sorrow by my letter, I do not regret it. Though I did regret it—I see that my letter hurt you, but only for a little while—yet now I am happy, not because you were made sorry, but because your sorrow led you to repentance" (2 Cor. 7:8–9).

Repentance is a "godly sorrow" (2 Cor. 7:11) that is brought about by the work of the Holy Spirit in us to chasten us toward maturity. By confession and repentance, we are made sensitive to the Spirit's work in our lives and are better able to respond to the conviction of the Spirit when we sin.

Pastor Jack struggles with pornography. He is not addicted, but looking at pornographic images brings him a false sense of comfort when he experiences stress. When he falls into sin, confession often takes two forms: one, he confesses his sin to the Lord in prayer and asks for forgiveness, and two, he confesses his sin to an older minister who disciples him. Jack experienced genuine godly sorrow, turning from counterfeit comfort in pornography to forgiveness and a reinvigorated relationship with the Lord and with his wife. Jack realizes that he is not flawless in this struggle, but he knows what it means to repent, to turn away from that which displeases the Lord and hampers his discipleship. He knows what it means to repent again and again. He lives in gospel hope.

Both types of repentance are brought about by the ministry of the Holy Spirit, who enables us to confess and to repent—again and again throughout our lives as we encounter sin that entangles us.

## CULTIVATION OF PERSONAL HOLINESS

Confession and repentance cultivate personal holiness. Intentional inner development yields a changed and changing life, in which one becomes more like Christ. Holiness is the strengthening by the Spirit "in your inner being, so that Christ may dwell in your hearts through faith" (Eph. 3:16–17). "Holiness" may not be a popular word in contemporary evangelical culture, but it is the essence of personal discipleship. We want to become increasingly more like Christ.

Peter acknowledged the struggle his readers had as they determined to grow toward Christlikeness. He urged them: "Therefore, with minds that are alert and fully sober, set your hope on the grace to be brought to you when Jesus Christ is revealed at his coming. As obedient children, do not conform to the evil desires you had when you lived in ignorance. But just as he who called you is holy, so be holy in all you do; for it is written: 'Be holy, because I am holy'" (1 Pet. 1:13–16).

Likewise, Paul underscored for Timothy, his son in the faith, the importance of diligent personal holiness because such intentionality has an impact not only personally on the preacher but also on the listener and all those who see his life: "Watch your life and doctrine closely," Paul urged. "Persevere in them, because if you do, you will save both yourself and your hearers" (1 Tim. 4:16). Puritan Richard Baxter encouraged pastors in his day and now: "Take heed to yourselves, lest your example contradict your doctrine, and lest you lay such stumbling blocks before the blind, as may the occasion be of their ruin; lest you unsay with your lives, what you say with your tongues; and be the greatest hinderers of the success of your own labours."[13]

James Wilhoit reminds us, "Holiness does not come simply from avoiding certain actions, but by our becoming a channel for God's empowering presence—living as a pipe, not a bucket." He continues, "Holiness begins with our being made new by God and grows as we open ourselves to the work of God."[14]

13. Richard Baxter, *The Reformed Pastor* (Edinburgh: Banner of Truth, 1979), 63.
14. James C. Wilhoit, *Spiritual Formation as if the Church Mattered: Growing in Christ through Community* (Grand Rapids: Baker Academic, 2008), 161.

Holiness is revealed in the life of a person who maintains a solid ongoing relationship with God. Holiness is the character transformation that takes place over the course of our lives as we mature in Christ, shaped by intentional inner development. "In an earlier age," observes Wilhoit, "holiness was seen as something possessing substance—a transcendent quality that flowed out of our deep inner essence, from our very souls."[15] Preachers, we want to be deep, long-term followers of Christ who cultivate lives of compelling holiness that evidence the work of Christ in us and through us. This is depth. This is substance.

For Pastor Mark, holiness means a steady, constant daily walk with God. Of course, this does not mean that Mark has it all together, but Mark affirms the apostle Paul's words to the Galatian Christians: "Since we live by the Spirit, let us keep in step with the Spirit" (Gal. 5:25). This means keeping himself in check throughout the day by confession of and repentance from the "fleshly desires" (Gal. 5:17–21). He can also take a personal spiritual inventory and chart how he has grown over the years as a believer by asking: "How have I grown in the last year in holiness? How different am I from when I first believed? What are the markers of maturity in my life?" As he cultivates a life of holiness, he knows he will benefit, and so will his congregation.

## The Way of Prayer

The preacher fosters the way of prayer. The intentional inner life of the preacher cannot thrive without prayer. I describe our relationship with God in prayer as the "way" of prayer. There are no formulas or quick-ways-to-growth prayers. Prayer is a way, a road, a route, a street, a pathway, a journey on which we walk with the Lord. The inner life of the preacher is nurtured by an ongoing conversation with the Father, Son, and Holy Spirit along the entire way of his or her life in Christ. Prayer is not episodic; it is the entire movie. Prayer provides a way toward growth and a relationship with God.

The way of prayer demonstrates one's dependence on the Lord. There is not a moment that you could exist without his presence and grace. Prayer concedes your utter reliance on God. We cannot do anything without God. Nothing. Nada. No how. Zilch. Prayer is our hand reaching to heaven to be held by the hand of God. We are linked to God in prayer by his love. We express in our prayers the words of need, hope, help, praise, trust, and thanks. God supplies all our needs in Christ Jesus—and our prayers formulate the expression of our relationship with him (Phil. 4:19).

15. Wilhoit, *Spiritual Formation as if the Church Mattered*, 162.

Since prayer is a way, a conversational and relational journey with the God of the universe, prayer is constant and continual, a moment-by-moment experience and practice. When Paul told the Thessalonian Christians to "pray continually" (1 Thess. 5:17), he meant it, for this is what God wants us to do! To pray always is to pray along the way, to enjoy a lifelong conversation with the Lord.

A specific prayer is to ask God to cultivate in us solid Christian character. When we purposefully speak with the Lord about our spiritual maturity, we place our growth at the center of our attention and God's consideration.

Praying for spiritual maturity is part of my practice of daily prayer. For most of my Christian life, starting when I was a freshman in college, I have kept a prayer list. The list includes family members, those who do not know the Savior, various ministries, people whom I mentor, friends, government leaders from local to national levels, and other matters of concern. When I pray for myself, I ask the Lord for wisdom and for maturity in Christ. I ask this daily. Having been a pastor and now a seminary professor, I have not escaped being a disciple of Jesus Christ. The word "disciple" means "learner" or "pupil." I will always be a disciple until the day I die or the Lord returns. I do not want to stop learning and growing and becoming more like the person that God calls me to be. Even in my sixties and in my positions of responsibility, I remain nothing more than a follower of Jesus Christ. I am still on my way.

The practice of prayer is a conversation with the Almighty in which we come to terms with who we really are—dependent disciples all our lives, all along the way.

## BIBLE READING AS IMMERSION IN THE SCRIPTURES

Whatever you choose to call the practice of Scripture reading—your devotions, Bible reading, your daily watch, or your time with God—reading God's Word strengthens the preacher's inner life. Although the Israelites were fed with manna, God reminded them that humans do not "live on bread alone but on every word that comes from the mouth of the LORD" (Deut. 8:3). This Word is our authority as preachers—and as disciples of Jesus Christ. Pastor Lee Eclov reflects on the immense value it is to a preacher to be fed by Christ through the reading of the Bible. Eclov ponders:

> Grace feeds on grace. If pastors are to dispense grace every time we turn around, then we need to take in grace the way runners take in carbs before a marathon. Jesus is our manna, our living grace, the bread of heaven. When we don't get enough of Christ we get spiritually lightheaded and weak in the knees. What's worse than weakness is that pastors who are not nourished by Christ's grace get

crotchety, indifferent, or suspicious around God's people. We take on a Pharisee scowl every time people don't perform. Our flocks stop seeing Jesus through us.[16]

I do not want to nag, cajole, or guilt anyone into reading the Scriptures daily. Nor do I intend to make you feel uneasy when you prayerfully and thoughtfully reflect on the Scripture passage on which you will be preaching the next week or in the future and consider this your daily reading. A devotional reflection on the preaching text accomplishes what Haddon Robinson detailed in his definition of biblical preaching: "the communication of a biblical concept, derived from and transmitted through a historical, grammatical, and literary study of a passage in its context, which the Holy Spirit first applies to the personality and experience of the preacher, then through the preacher, applies to the hearers."[17] Here the preacher strives to cooperate with the Holy Spirit to apply the truth of the text in the preacher's life. Only then will the preaching text connect with the listener.

On the other hand, we may be tempted to treat the Bible strictly as a sermon-preparation resource. Even when we are reflecting on and praying through a Bible passage on a given day, we might look at every text we read for potential sermon material, therefore avoiding the life-shaping effect of Scripture reading.

Aside from this caution, Bible reading enriches our Scripture vocabulary and helps us to have a conversation across the Testaments, in interaction with doctrines, and in application. "The B-I-B-L-E," goes the children's song. "That's the book for me!" It continues, "I stand alone on the Word of God, the B-I-B-L-E!" This is all we have to preach—not about our experiences, not about us, but about the Word and the giver of this Word. Pastor Zack Eswine reminds us about the key role of the Bible in our lives as preachers. Eswine urges, "We open the book to behold not it but him as he is revealed to us in it."[18]

Pastoral ministry is unpredictable and life itself is fickle. When we talk about Bible reading and other practices that shape our character, it is easy to be overcome by guilt. "I missed reading my Bible today and even yesterday. Will God not bless me in my preaching and teaching?" Hardly. The Sovereign of the universe is aware of your plight. You have not fallen into hypocrisy or heresy. You simply missed a day or days of reading your Bible. The challenges of hospital calls, Bible studies, home visitations, the death of a church member,

---

16. Lee Eclov, *Pastoral Graces: Reflections on the Care of Souls* (Chicago: Moody, 2012), 131.

17. Haddon W. Robinson, *Biblical Preaching: The Development and Delivery of Expository Messages*, 3rd ed. (Grand Rapids: Baker Academic, 2014), 12.

18. Zack Eswine, *The Imperfect Pastor: Discovering Joy in Our Limitations through a Daily Apprenticeship with Jesus* (Wheaton: Crossway, 2015), 164.

the unexpected counseling session for a distressed couple, and sick kids at home are not going to hamper your long-term relationship with God. Bible reading immerses us in Scripture so that we can be nourished from it when we face challenging moments in ministry and in our preaching. Regular Scripture reading gives us the foundation for ministry over the long haul.

### Intentional Inter-Development

The preacher fosters personal intentional inner development, the nurturing of a relationship with Jesus Christ, beholding him and being shaped by the promise of the gospel by confession, repentance, holiness, prayer, and Bible reading. Likewise, inter-development turns from the inside to the outside, considering growth that takes place as one engages and interacts with other believers. Maturity is advanced through what can be called a wide discipleship that takes place in the local church and through specific individual discipleship relationships.

## Intentional Inter-Development in the Local Church

My observation as a pastor and as a seminary professor is that discipleship is the missing link in the church. For some reason or another, discipleship is considered to be more of a program than a lens through which the church carries out its mission. Discipleship is something churches have left to campus ministries to define or for youth groups to experience but not for the church in all of its textured mission to define and experience. I want to change your perspective on ministry, on the mission of the church, and on what it means for you to be a pastor and preacher of the gospel—and the change has to do with discipleship.

Intentional inter-development means that we are committed to the church, that we are on board with its mission of making disciples. This means that we believe in the strategic role of the local church—large or small—to transform lives with the hope of the gospel that shapes men and women and boys and girls into the likeness of Christ. We are part of this sometimes messy mission as members of the church and as pastors of the church. J. R. Woodward and Dan White Jr. say it plainly: "Don't be fooled by church attendance. Unless people are on an intentional discipleship path they will not be shaped for God's mission in the world."[19]

My life has been dramatically shaped by the discipleship mission of the local church, both as a young person who received a call into ministry and

19. J. R. Woodward and Dan White Jr., *The Church as Movement: Starting and Sustaining Missional-Incarnational Communities* (Downers Grove, IL: InterVarsity, 2016), 89.

as a pastor. My home church lived out discipleship. As a young boy I came to faith out of a non-Christian home. Older, mature-in-the-faith men and women invited me into their lives and homes. The Sunday school teaching, youth group, and preaching from the pulpit had a cumulative discipleship effect that matured me and gave me the confidence to trust the Lord for the call he placed on my life to preach. The church affirmed my call with the responsibilities given to me and confirmed my gifts at my ordination. This small country church sent me off to seminary and paid for most of my costs with checks from the members of this faithful flock.

Funny thing is, they probably did not realize what they were doing. They did not call what they did "discipleship." Their faithfulness to the gospel and following Jesus's command to make disciples was like wool that grows on the backs of sheep. They did not recognize that it was happening. This small Baptist congregation was not perfect—far from it. But congregants took nurturing believers seriously. This is the inter-development that we want to cultivate in our lives, in our understanding of ministry, and in the churches we serve. As Mark Dever underscores, "The church has an obligation to be God's means of growing people in grace. Mature, holiness-seeking influences in a covenant community of believers can be tools in God's hand for growing his people. As God's people are built up and grow together in holiness and self-giving love, they should improve their ability to administer discipline and to encourage discipleship."[20]

As a pastor, having discipleship as the template for ministry has given me focus and purpose. I can determine the spiritual age of my congregation and preach to it, planning sermons that move them to maturity.[21] When I, together with the leadership of the church, can see where the church is spiritually, we can then strategize prayerfully about how preaching and other aspects of ministry can mature the faith of the congregation.

Even though we are shepherding the congregation to maturity, we too experience the grace of the gospel as we benefit from the mutual nurturing that takes place in the church. Pastor Paul underscored this in his letter to the Philippian church. He thanked God for their "partnership [fellowship] in the gospel from the first day until now" (Phil. 1:5). Paul and the church were all too familiar with their shared life from the beginning till the time at which he wrote his letter to them—and he thanked God for this solidarity of purpose and experience in living out the gospel together. We too participate in this in the churches we serve.

20. Mark Dever, *What Is a Healthy Church?* (Wheaton: Crossway, 2005), 108–9.
21. A detailed exploration of preaching as discipleship is given in my book *Preaching with a Plan: Sermon Strategies for Growing Mature Believers* (Grand Rapids: Baker Books, 2012).

Of course, in our experience of the church's conjoined life in Christ, the practices of confession, repentance, holiness, prayer, and Bible reading are brought to a new level. It may be in the local church that we first came to faith and among those believers we confessed our sin, repented of a former life, started on the road to holiness, and began nurturing a life of prayer and Scripture reading in the context of discipleship. Here, these practices move from an inner practice to an inter-engagement. Confession takes place in the liturgy of gathered worship. Sometimes confession is the public renouncing of sin, as encouraged by the apostle James: "Therefore confess your sins to each other and pray for each other so that you may be healed" (James 5:16). Here our repentance is tested. Fellow believers can see by how we live if indeed we have turned from that which used to pull us down. We are taught to pray by the example of other believers. We are encouraged to imbibe the Scriptures for nourishment and growth.

As preachers, we care for our inter-growth by committing to the local church as the means of discipleship. But there is more to this devotion. There is another level to intentional inter-development. This aspect drills down from a wider discipleship to a personal discipleship.

### Intentional Inter-Development in Discipleship

Life in Christ is not like being a golfer. The golfer is alone. She has no team. Everything depends on her to make it. Christianity is a team sport. We are following Christ together, which is the mission and purpose of the church. There are members of the team, and they are all different. Some of them require specific exercises to continue to develop. Not every team member is the same. Each needs different kinds of help. Each needs various strategies of coaching.

We see glimpses of inter-development in discipleship throughout Scripture with Moses and Aaron, Elijah and Elisha, John the Baptist and his followers, Jesus and his disciples, Paul and Timothy, and Paul and Titus, among many other examples.

"Go and make disciples of all nations," commands the risen Jesus to his disciples. The disciples that Jesus's disciples were commanded to make were not simply to be converted to faith in Christ but, Jesus orders, were to be taught "to obey everything I have commanded you" (Matt. 28:16–20). These new converts were to be shaped into followers of Jesus by learning his teachings—the Scriptures. Older believers nurturing younger believers is part of the process of discipleship. Elders and older women are to teach those younger in the faith (1 Tim. 3:2; Titus 2:3–5). Paul tells Titus that elders "must hold firmly to the trustworthy message as it has been taught, so that [they] can encourage others by sound doctrine and refute those who oppose it" (Titus 1:9). Face-to-face discipleship is at the heart of gospel growth.

What does this matter to preachers? We may nod our heads in agreement to the idea of discipleship on a wider scale in the church, but when it comes to being discipled ourselves and intentionally discipling others, we may draw the line. But if the lens of ministry is discipleship, then the field of vision includes us as well.

I am grateful for the men and women whom God has placed in my life who have discipled me. From the time I became a believer in junior high school to the present, I have been receiving instruction that has shaped my character for Christ. Pastor LeVan led me to Christ and poured his life into me as a young person and as a seminarian, shaping me into a pastor with his love and care. Dale and Frances Currie opened their hearts and their home to me as a new convert from a non-Christian home. They taught me from their lives and from the Scriptures what it means to live life, demonstrating to me the contours of a Christian marriage. Pastor Bickley saw to it to delay his retirement until I finished seminary so he could oversee my ordination. Beth and Jim Ray invited me into their lives, and we studied the Bible together weekly in their home, but I got to see much more than biblical truth—I saw how they lived hospitable lives with love. I cannot forget Ken Swetland, who has been a Paul to me for over thirty-five years throughout my time as a seminarian, a pastor, and now a professor. For over twenty years Haddon Robinson and I shared the responsibility of teaching preaching. Haddon's interest in my life as a follower of Christ went well beyond the classroom. I am forever grateful for his impress on my life and for the ways in which he discipled me.

Not only have I experienced discipleship, but I also practice it. From my days as a camp counselor through my time as a pastor and seminary professor, discipleship is the lens through which I have viewed my ministry. Since becoming a professor I have met with seminarians preparing for the pastorate. Every year the Lord leads into my life men with whom I meet weekly. Typically, they come to our home for dinner—one of them at a time. My wife, Rhonda, who is also committed to discipleship, joins me in opening our home to them throughout the three years they are in seminary. Someone's feet are under our table for dinner at least three nights a week. Following the meal, we will excuse ourselves and go to the den to talk, study Scripture, discuss a book, delve into our lives, and pray together. The relationship the men and I have does not stop when they graduate. I tell them, "You now have me for the rest of your life." Not a day goes by that I do not hear from one of them. I have preached at their ordinations, conducted their weddings, counseled them in their marriages, and walked with them through their divorces and personal difficulties. I hope they benefit from our relationship. I know that I do. I love them. I am constantly challenged in my growth in Christ because of intentional inter-development in discipleship.

If we embrace the concept that Christ's mission for us is one of discipleship, we need to make intentional steps to enlist someone to mentor and disciple us. Do whatever it takes to cultivate a relationship with someone more mature in the faith who will encourage you to move forward in confession, repentance, holiness, prayer, and Bible reading—in discipleship. This is genuine gospel growth, growth that all preachers require to bring balance to their personal world.

What are the indicators of maturity in any believer's life, but especially in the life of a preacher? We turn to explore these characteristics in the final section.


## Markers of Christian Maturity

What are the characteristics that distinguish a maturing disciple of Jesus Christ, one whose character is being shaped by confession, repentance, holiness, prayer, and Scripture reading in the crucible of discipleship? These characteristics are the markers of maturity, the biblical qualities that make an impress into a preacher's life. These might even be called "gospel virtues,"[22] the mature contours of grace imaged in a believer's life as demonstrated in the way a believer thinks and acts.

Below is a provisional list from the Bible of character qualities that maturing disciples can aspire to, pray for, be nurtured in and discipled toward, develop in the Christian community, and demonstrate in their own lives.

**Markers of Christian Maturity**
"By this everyone will know that you are my disciples,
if you love one another."
John 13:35

- One who observes the Ten Commandments in light of the new covenant (Exod. 20:1–17; Deut. 5:6–22; Lev. 19:18; Matt. 19:16–22)
- Wise (Proverbs; Acts 6:1–6; James 1:5; 3:17; on Jesus as the epitome of wisdom, see Luke 2:40; Matt. 13:54; Mark 6:2; Col. 1:15–20; 2:3; John 1:1–3)
- Poor in spirit (Matt. 5:3)

---

22. A phrase used by Jim Wilhoit in his discussion on holiness. Wilhoit, *Spiritual Formation as if the Church Mattered*, 162.

- One who mourns over sin (Matt. 5:4)
- Meek (Matt. 5:5; Ps. 37:11)
- One who hungers and thirsts for righteousness (Matt. 5:6)
- Merciful (Matt. 5:7; Luke 6:36; James 2:13; Jude 22)
- Pure in heart (Matt. 5:8; Ps. 73:1)
- A peacemaker (Matt. 5:9)
- Full of the Spirit (Acts 6:1–6; Eph. 5:18)
- One whose mind is renewed (Rom. 12:2; Phil. 4:8–9; 2 Pet. 1:5)
- Spiritually gifted (Rom. 12:3–8; 1 Cor. 12:1–11)

  - Prophesying
  - Serving
  - Teaching
  - Encouraging
  - Contributing to the needs of others
  - Leadership
  - Mercy
  - Wisdom
  - Knowledge (2 Pet. 3:18)
  - Faith
  - Healing
  - Possesses miraculous powers
  - Distinguishes between spirits
  - Speaks in different tongues
  - Interprets tongues

- One who exhibits the fruit of the Spirit (Gal. 5:22–26)

  - Love (John 13:35; Rom. 12:9; 2 Pet. 1:7)
  - Joy (Neh. 8:10; John 15:11; 17:13; Rom. 15:13; 1 Thess. 1:6; Heb. 1:9; James 1:2; 1 Pet. 1:8; Jude 24)
  - Peace
  - Patience
  - Kindness (2 Pet. 1:7)
  - Goodness (2 Pet. 1:5)
  - Faithfulness

- ○ Gentleness
- ○ Self-control (2 Pet. 1:6)

- Prayerful (Matt. 6:5–15; Phil. 4:6; Col. 4:2; 1 Thess. 5:17)
- Above reproach (1 Tim. 3:2)
- Faithful to one spouse (1 Tim. 3:2; Titus 1:6)
- Temperate (1 Tim. 3:2)
- Self-controlled (1 Tim. 3:2)
- Respectable (1 Tim. 3:2)
- Hospitable (1 Tim. 3:2; Rom. 12:13; 1 Tim. 5:10; 1 Pet. 4:9; 3 John 8)
- Able to teach (1 Tim. 3:2; 2 Tim. 2:24)
- Not given to drunkenness (1 Tim. 3:3; Titus 2:3)
- Not violent but gentle (1 Tim. 3:3; 2 Cor. 10:1; Gal. 5:23; Col. 3:12; 1 Tim. 6:11; 1 Pet. 3:15)
- Not quarrelsome (1 Tim. 3:3)
- Not a lover of money (1 Tim. 3:3; Luke 16:13; 1 Tim. 6:10; Heb. 13:5; 1 Pet. 5:2)
- One who manages the household well (1 Tim. 3:4; Titus 1:6–7)
- Not overbearing (Titus 1:7)
- Not a recent convert (1 Tim. 3:6)
- One who has a good reputation with outsiders (community, nonbelievers) (1 Tim. 3:7)
- Sincere (1 Tim. 3:8)
- Not given to the pursuit of dishonest gain (1 Tim. 3:8)
- Blameless (1 Tim. 3:10; Titus 1:6)
- Not a malicious talker but temperate (1 Tim. 3:11)
- Trustworthy (1 Tim. 3:11)
- One who demonstrates perseverance (2 Pet. 1:6)
- Godly (2 Pet. 1:6)

These biblical markers provide a broad template for character formation and development for the church and for the preacher. They provide the contours of discipleship by directing our attention to the One whom we desire to emulate and through whose hand the Holy Spirit is shaping us—inscribing on and in us the characteristics of the kingdom. Klaus Issler's words are helpful: "While objectively true, moral rules are not our ultimate reference point."

He emphasizes: "Jesus himself is the ultimate reference point for us. We look to Jesus' own authoritative example and illustrations that present a range of ways to love God. We believe correctly that Jesus is central to salvation, as Scripture teaches. Likewise, Jesus is central to sanctification, to discipleship, to Christian ethics, as Jesus himself teaches."[23]

The preacher's personal world is shaped by intentional inner development and inter-development that show the contours of gospel growth as demonstrated in the markers of maturity within the context of discipleship.

## Conclusion

This chapter has focused on the personal world of the preacher. Developing our personal world allows us to be an instrument of the gospel in the lives of others. Only then will we be as effective as we can be for the gospel. Sure, we may study preaching—the techniques, steps, sermon shapes, listener analysis, gestures, and pacing—but these are what people see on the outside as we preach the sermon. The sermon is much more than what listeners hear and see. Dave McClellan urges: "This is why, to really preach better, we can't fixate simply on preaching. There are other more weighty issues in play, things we must look in the eye. We must face our struggling marriages, our poor work ethic, our desperate lack of compassion, our hiding and blaming. A dishonest, angry, or negligent preacher will never produce a grounded sermon no matter how many commentaries are consulted. We cannot escape ourselves, and until we face ourselves, our preaching cannot help but suffer."[24]

Our personal world will transform—and we will begin to transform—when we take stock of it with an honest examination of ourselves. Oswald Chambers says that is the place to begin. Chambers writes:

> The lives of others are examples for us, but God requires us to examine our own souls. It is slow work—so slow that it takes God all of time and eternity to make a man or woman conform to His purpose. We can only be used by God after we allow Him to show us the deep, hidden areas of our own character. It is astounding how ignorant we are about ourselves! We don't even recognize the envy, laziness, or pride within us when we see it. But Jesus will reveal to us everything we have held within ourselves before His grace began to work. How many of us have learned to look inwardly with courage?

23. Klaus Issler, *Living into the Life of Jesus: The Formation of Christian Character* (Downers Grove, IL: InterVarsity, 2012), 21.

24. McClellan, *Preaching by Ear*, 45.

We have to get rid of the idea that we understand ourselves. That is always the last bit of pride to go. The only One who understands us is God. The greatest curse in our spiritual life is pride. If we have ever had a glimpse of what we are like in the sight of God, we will never say, "Oh, I'm so unworthy." We will understand that this goes without saying. But as long as there is any doubt that we are unworthy, God will continue to close us in until He gets us alone. Whenever there is any element of pride or conceit remaining, Jesus can't teach us anything. He will allow us to experience heartbreak or the disappointment we feel when our intellectual pride is wounded. He will reveal numerous misplaced affections or desires—things over which we never thought He would have to get us alone. Many things are shown to us, often without effect. But when God gets us alone over them, they will be clear.[25]

The preacher's personal world impacts his or her preaching. This cannot help but be the case. Why? It has to do with character. "Character builds sermons," says McClellan.[26] He is right. We want to cultivate our character by putting into practice these gospel virtues of confession, repentance, and holiness—these nurture us toward the markers of Christian maturity in the context of discipleship. When we do, our personal world will be changed, and the ministry that God has given to us will be transformed and strengthened too. And maybe, just maybe, God will choose to use us as a mouthpiece that will edify his people and glorify his name.

25. Oswald Chambers, *My Utmost for His Highest*, ed. James Reimann (Grand Rapids: Discovery House, 1992), reading for January 12.
26. McClellan, *Preaching by Ear*, 45.

# 5

## The World of Ethnic and Cultural Issues in Preaching

MATTHEW D. KIM

### Introduction

The concept of race has historically served as a social construct to classify persons based on their physical/biological features.[1] However, race is the larger umbrella for what we commonly think of as ethnic and cultural differences. We live in a heavily racialized world in which race and ethnicity are often attached to basic elements in life that were not originally equated with racial or ethnic labels, such as the racialization of work or of politics.[2] But are we

---

Sections of this chapter have been employed and adapted from my article "A Blindspot in Homiletics: Preaching That Exegetes Ethnicity," *Journal of the Evangelical Homiletics Society* 11, no. 1 (March 2011): 66–83. Used by permission. I also incorporate some select ideas from my book *Preaching with Cultural Intelligence: Understanding the People Who Hear Our Sermons* (Grand Rapids: Baker Academic, 2017), particularly from chap. 6, which is on preaching and ethnicity.

1. Audrey Smedley, "The History of the Idea of Race . . . and Why It Matters" (paper presented at "Race, Human Variation and Disease: Consensus and Frontiers" conference, American Anthropological Association, Warrenton, VA, March 2007), available at www.understandingrace.org/resources/pdf/disease/smedley.pdf.

2. Terms like "racialization" or "racialized" have become normative in sociology. See Michael Omi and Howard Winant, *Racial Formation in the United States: From the 1960s to the 1980s*, 3rd ed. (New York: Routledge, 2014), 142.

truly living in a post-racial society in which we have overcome racial barriers? The election of the first African American president in our nation's history in 2008 made it seem that racial equality for all Americans was an imminent reality. To the contrary, however, we have witnessed mounting racial tensions, perhaps at an all-time high, as evidenced by the chorus of recurring acts of discrimination, hate crimes, and shootings of ethnic minorities, especially African Americans.[3]

Preachers are students of cultures—biblical cultures as well as contemporary ones. Perhaps more than ever, ethnicity, culture, and cultural differences have wedged themselves into the homiletical equation, so that preachers need to consider especially those listeners who diverge ethnically and culturally from themselves. Preachers cannot afford to disengage from or to be disinterested any longer in the cultural and ethnic demographics represented in their neighborhoods, congregations, and beyond. This ethnic and cultural engagement will require preachers to intentionally explore the world of ethnicity and culture via open-mindedness, sensitivity, and valuing persons who do not share their ethnic and cultural backgrounds.

While the Bible does not explicitly address the concept of race per se, it clearly acknowledges the world of different ethnic groups and their respective cultures.[4] In this chapter, my goal is to initiate a conversation that we seldom have with respect to sermon preparation and proclamation, a conversation that concerns ethnicity and culture.[5] My desire here is to discuss some of the challenges and opportunities we have in preaching regarding ethnic and cultural concerns.

Space limitations will curtail this discussion to three aspects of this subject. First, the world of ethnic and cultural issues must be couched within a candid discussion of the past with respect to a biblical understanding of ethnicity, as well as our shared immigration history in the United States. Second, we will identify some of the current dilemmas preachers face collectively in light of communicating within the confines of ethnic and cultural spaces. Third, we want to identify practical ways to encourage ethnic and cultural exploration and integration in our preaching today and into the future. But, to know the future, we must first understand the past.

3. See my *Preaching with Cultural Intelligence: Understanding the People Who Hear Our Sermons* (Grand Rapids: Baker Academic, 2017), chap. 6.

4. For help in understanding biblical ethnicities and cultures, see Bill T. Arnold and Brent A. Strawn, eds., *The World around the Old Testament: The People and Places of the Ancient Near East* (Grand Rapids: Baker Academic, 2016).

5. See my "A Blindspot in Homiletics: Preaching That Exegetes Ethnicity," *Journal of the Evangelical Homiletics Society* 11, no. 1 (March 2011): 66–83.

## Ethnicity and the World of History

Where did the concept of ethnicity come from? We should begin with the world of the Bible. Biblically speaking, ethnicity and ethnic identity in Scripture have often been portrayed with the following dichotomy: there are the Jews (God's chosen people) and there is everyone else. Growing up in the church, if ethnicity (namely, the creation of different ethnicities) was ever mentioned from the pulpit, preachers referenced two different Bible texts. First, some preachers referenced Genesis 9 and the narrative about the sons of Noah, contending that every ethnic group in existence today can trace its ancestry to the three sons of Noah: Shem, Ham, and Japheth. Second, preachers often ascribed the formation of different ethnicities to the by-product of the sin of pride exhibited in the Tower of Babel narrative in Genesis 11, whereby the people at Shinar decided to make a name for themselves and build a great tower for their glory. In employing either of these texts, preachers have explicated God's creation of ethnic differences as the consequence of judgment for sins committed. This has contributed to the belief among certain Christians that the genesis of ethnic diversity resulted from acts of sin and a fallen humanity rather than from God's sovereign purposes and pleasure.

A contrasting view is suggested in an article from the Ethics and Religious Liberty Commission, in which the author writes this rebuttal to such commonly held beliefs:

> It will be noted in a careful reading of the passage that: (1) God placed a curse on no one; (2) Noah did the cursing after having awakened from a drunken stupor; (3) Canaan was the one actually cursed by Noah, not Ham; (4) there is no indication of God having approved Noah's act or of His having implemented it in any way; and (5) no reference is made to anyone being turned any color different from what he already was. [In addition] Genesis 11:1–9 records the incident when God confounded the builders of the tower of Babel but not one word is said about race, and the concept of race is not in the passage.[6]

In my search to understand the earliest evidence of ethnic consciousness and ethnic identity in the Bible, I have found myself drawn to Genesis 10—what is known as the Table of Nations. Beginning in Genesis 10:4, Moses identifies the sons of Javan, a descendant of Japheth, as "Elishah, Tarshish, the Kittites and the Rodanites." William Mounce explains verse 5: "From these the maritime peoples (*goyim*) spread out into their territories by their clans

---

6. See "The Bible Speaks on Race," Ethics and Religious Liberty Commission, January 24, 2006, http://mail.erlc.com/article/the-bible-speaks-on-race.

(*mispaha*) within their nations (*goyim*), each with its own language [*lason*]."[7] In similar terms, after listing the descendants of Ham, Genesis 10:20 reads, "These are the sons of Ham by their clans and languages, in their territories and nations." Finally, Genesis 10:31 reads: "These are the sons of Shem by their clans and languages, in their territories and nations." The four distinguishing characteristics among the descendants of Shem, Ham, and Japheth regarding clan, language, territory, and nation seem to indicate that at some point in Noah's sons' generational lineages different ethnic groups took shape, as we currently understand the terms "ethnicities" or "people groups." However, nowhere does Scripture specifically spell out that the creation of different ethnicities was God's enactment of judgment for sins.

Instead of condemnation for sin, God's Word seems to suggest that nations, peoples, or ethnic groups were created for his joy and pleasure. How different ethnic groups originated is of interest to people but appears to be out of the purview of Scripture. The bookends of the Bible, Genesis and Revelation, communicate God's plan and pleasure in creating diversity. As Genesis 1:27 reads: "So God created man in his own image, in the image of God he created them; male and female he created them." Surely God was referring not only to Adam and Eve but also to the entirety of the human race. All humans in history have been and are created in his image. Similarly, in Revelation 7:9–10, the apostle John writes: "After this I looked, and there before me was a great multitude that no one could count, from every nation, tribe, people and language, standing before the throne and before the Lamb. They were wearing white robes and were holding palm branches in their hands. And they cried out in a loud voice: 'Salvation belongs to our God, who sits on the throne, and to the Lamb.'" Therefore, God does not reserve places in heaven only for those belonging to a few *choice* ethnic groups—for example, Jews and Greeks alone. Rather, God desires worship from all types of people (i.e., ethnic groups) as they enter eternity with him. While God does not show partiality, as it says in Acts 10:34 and Romans 2:11, the problem we face is that as fallen human beings, we demonstrate ethnic prejudice and express partiality toward our own ethnic group.

Having briefly explored Scripture's perspective on ethnicity, let's draw closer to the present reality. Historians of the United States and even the late president John F. Kennedy remind us that America has always been "a nation of immigrants."[8] For centuries, ethnic groups have migrated across oceans

---

7. William D. Mounce, ed., *Mounce's Complete Expository Dictionary of Old and New Testament Words* (Grand Rapids: Zondervan, 2006), 465; see also page 112 for clans (*mispaha*) and page 391 for language (*lason*).

8. See John F. Kennedy, *A Nation of Immigrants*, rev. ed. (New York: Harper & Row, 1964).

to arrive on what is now claimed as US soil. For each passing generation of Anglos or whites, children of European immigrants typically dissolved their association with their family's ethnic heritage, culture, and language to embrace a broader national American identity.[9] This common racial identity of "being white" became the norm of what a "true" American was and is.[10]

White Americans can, as sociologist Herbert J. Gans explained, choose to adopt a "symbolic ethnicity"[11] via celebrating cultural holidays and traditions like wearing the color green on St. Patrick's Day, eating cultural cuisine like the Polish pierogi, or practicing cultural traditions, such as men of Scottish ancestry wearing kilts or German Americans enjoying their selection of dunkel beers during Oktoberfest. For Anglos, thinking about one's ethnicity is usually optional.[12]

However, ethnicity is not "symbolic" for non-Anglos such as Africans, Latinos, Native Americans, Arabs, and Asians, who do not have the luxury to choose a general American identity due to their race, ethnicity, and skin color. Ethnic minorities in America have regularly encountered prejudice and exclusion.[13] Moreover, many ethnic minorities cannot escape from discrimination, since we are not considered to be "real" Americans by the dominant culture. Just think how many times this type of social interaction has occurred: "Where are you from?" asks the majority-culture person. The minority person responds, "San Francisco." To which the majority person probes incredulously, "No, where are you *really* from?" We are never considered to be insiders but remain "forever foreigners."[14]

Historians record three major waves of how American sociologists envisioned this country handling ethnic and cultural diversity: Anglo conformity, the melting pot, and cultural pluralism.[15] In 1964, Milton Gordon first described Anglo conformity as a cultural group's relinquishment of the ethnic or immigrant culture in favor of a widespread and dominant European or Anglo

9. Richard D. Alba, *Ethnic Identity: The Transformation of White America* (New Haven: Yale University Press, 1990), 3.

10. See Paula Harris and Doug Schaupp, *Being White: Finding Our Place in a Multiethnic World* (Downers Grove, IL: InterVarsity, 2004).

11. Herbert J. Gans, "Symbolic Ethnicity: The Future of Ethnic Groups and Cultures in America," *Ethnic and Racial Studies* 2 (1979): 1–20.

12. Alba, *Ethnic Identity*, 138–39.

13. E.g., President Chester Arthur signed the Chinese Exclusion Act in 1882. See Joaquin Miller, "The Chinese and the Exclusion Act," *North American Review* 173, no. 541 (December 1901): 782–89.

14. See Mia Tuan, *Forever Foreigners or Honorary Whites? The Asian Ethnic Experience Today* (New Brunswick, NJ: Rutgers University Press, 2003).

15. See my *Preaching to Second Generation Korean Americans: Towards a Possible Selves Contextual Homiletic* (New York: Peter Lang, 2007), 24.

American cultural value system.[16] Anglo conformity or cultural assimilation is the norm where all races and ethnicities are expected to conform to the ways of the dominant group. The second wave, the melting-pot hypothesis, argued that various immigrant groups would eventually melt together to become a "new indigenous American type."[17] This category has been far from successful or achievable. Finally, cultural pluralism, or what some have called "the mosaic," believed that all ethnic groups would possess the freedom to maintain their own distinct ethnic and cultural identity in American society.[18]

In more than two centuries of American history, however, the overt and tacit expectations have always been that all immigrants and ethnic minorities would jettison their ethnicity and culture in order to fit in and become "American," even though the dominant culture has not always regarded them as equals. In her book *Preaching in an Age of Globalization*, Eunjoo Mary Kim writes, "Just as a salad dressing serves to weaken the distinctiveness of each ingredient by blending it with other ingredients, all thus acquiring the same flavor and taste, so the various members of multiethnic culture come together, blending their uniqueness with the dominant, controlling power of society."[19]

Even within evangelical Christian churches, ethnic minority persons are often expected to assimilate and become like the majority culture and play by the majority's rules and expectations. This expectation can be true in any church context in which there is a visible racial or ethnic majority, whether it's Anglo American, African American, Arab American, Asian American, Hispanic American, or Native American.

How, then, can we as preachers enable our listeners to enjoy their ethnicity and culture within a congregational culture that is predominantly monocultural? The first step is to understand ethnic identity and its extreme form: ethnocentrism.

## The World of Ethnic Identity and Ethnocentrism

How can we navigate these concepts of ethnic identity and ethnocentrism? What distinguishes these two perspectives? First of all, ethnic identity is an identification with one's own ethnic group. Individuals in your congregation

---

16. Milton Gordon, *Assimilation in American Life: The Role of Race, Religion, and National Origins* (New York: Oxford University Press, 1964), 85.

17. Gordon, *Assimilation in American Life*, 85. See also Kim, *Preaching to Second Generation Korean Americans*, 25.

18. Gordon, *Assimilation in American Life*, 38.

19. Eunjoo Mary Kim, *Preaching in an Age of Globalization* (Louisville: Westminster John Knox, 2010), 105.

will ascribe to high ethnic identification, low ethnic identification, or something in between.[20] A congregant who possesses high ethnic identity consciousness will maintain his or her culture (and perhaps even language) of origin rather than assimilate into the majority culture. By the same measure, persons with low ethnic identity subscribe to the culture and ways of the majority culture and relinquish the ethnic culture and perhaps even language of the country of their ethnic ancestry. Here, I must note that ethnicity and culture are distinct elements. For instance, one can be ethnically Spanish (one's ancestry of origin being Spain) but culturally Taiwanese (one's culture of residence living in Taiwan). That ethnically Spanish person may completely assimilate into Taiwanese culture, but he or she remains ethnically Spanish. Further, he or she may retain Spanish culture or may jettison it, depending on how many generations removed his or her family is from Spain, as well as other factors. Yes, this can be tricky to discern, but we want to remind ourselves that ethnicity and culture are not the same thing. That is, how one looks on the outside is not necessarily synonymous with one's culture, which is lived and breathed on the inside and expressed externally.

Ethnocentrism, on the other hand, is the belief that one's own ethnic group is superior to all others.[21] An early biblical example of the Jewish people's predilection toward ethnocentrism comes in the story of Genesis 24, in which Abraham commands his chief servant not to find a wife for Isaac among the Canaanite people. Yes, the Canaanites worshiped foreign idols, but there is also an undercurrent of ethnocentrism and ethnic prejudice against the Canaanites and other ethnic peoples. We observe a similar ethnocentrism in the next generation with Isaac commanding Jacob in Genesis 28:1 not to marry a Canaanite woman and Rebekah's distaste for Judith and Basemath, who were Esau's Hittite wives. Ethnocentrism is not always expressed strictly with regard to marriage, but allow me to carry the same illustration into the modern day.

As the son of Korean immigrants, ethnic identity and vestiges of ethnocentrism were instilled in me from an early age. When I was at the impressionable age of five, my mother asked me to repeat the following mantra: "I will marry a Korean Christian with a nice personality." During my teenage years, I remember being rejected by certain Caucasian girls. My father told me not to be depressed about any of these rejections. Rather, he responded, "Matt, look in the mirror. What do you see?" This was my dad's rhetorical device. "You are American by birth and citizenship, but your face is Korean. You will

20. See Harry H. L. Kitano and Roger Daniels, *Asian Americans: Emerging Minorities*, 3rd ed. (Upper Saddle River, NJ: Prentice-Hall, 2001), 212.

21. Patty Lane, *A Beginner's Guide to Crossing Cultures: Making Friends in a Multi-Cultural World* (Downers Grove, IL: InterVarsity, 2009), 38.

always be seen by whites as being Korean and not really American." With these reminders, my parents encouraged me to repeat this "marriage mantra" until the day I got married. Whom did I end up marrying? you ask. You guessed right. I married a Korean (American) Christian with a nice personality.

Ethnocentric behavior looks different across the spectrum of ethnicities and cultures. In general, ethnocentrism is heightened in cultures where a particular ethnic group has experienced oppression and occupation, such as the Korean people being occupied and oppressed by the Japanese in the early twentieth century. From 1910 to 1945, Koreans were prohibited from speaking their native language and forced to speak Japanese and practice Japanese customs. In view of ethnic identity and ethnocentrism, how are we to respond, especially in our preaching?

## Universal versus Particular Identities

A common approach to preaching about ethnic identity is to minimize its significance. The late C. Eric Lincoln and Lawrence Mamiya, professors of religion, differentiated between universal and particular identities. A universal identity is one's Christian identity, which usurps or transcends ethnicity, while a particular identity relates to a specific ethnic identity within an ethnic group, such as being Russian or Kenyan.[22] Using scriptural evidence, such as Galatians 3:28, that calls for a more universal identity in Christ rather than particular identities such as one's ethnicity or gender, some preachers will gravitate toward preaching on our universal Christian identity to the exclusion of all other identities, also known as "being color blind" in our preaching.

While I affirm that Christian identity is of the highest importance, we cannot escape the embodiment of our own skin. We live in an embodied state that is ethnic and for certain congregants even multiethnic and multicultural (e.g., biracial, multiracial, and living in numerous cultural contexts). In my doctoral work, I conducted the first research study on Asian American preaching. Specifically, my supervisors narrowed my research scope to second-generation Korean Americans. Fieldwork with Korean American preachers and listeners revealed that ethnicity and ethnic identity were rarely discussed in their sermons.[23] This omission of ethnic identity was largely for two reasons. First, whenever one ethnic minority group becomes a representative majority in a given context, the minority that is now a majority feels empowered not to

22. C. Eric Lincoln and Lawrence Mamiya, *The Black Church in the African American Experience* (Durham, NC: Duke University Press, 1990), 12.
23. Kim, *Preaching to Second Generation Korean Americans*, 172–75.

have to respond to their "otherness." Put differently, this ethnic church culture becomes a place where the minority no longer has to answer to the majority in society. They are free to be themselves. As mentioned above, ethnic identity or ethnic consciousness is not a choice for ethnic minorities, as it often is for white Americans.

Second, related to symbolic ethnicity, ethnic minorities like Korean Americans and others have been trained by white American seminary professors who acknowledge a common, universal Christian identity usually to the exclusion of particular ethnic identities primarily because ethnic identity is not at the forefront of white homileticians' minds and experiences. The same phenomenon may be true of multiethnic congregations, in which ethnicity is seldom discussed because of the common denominator that our universal identity is in Christ alone (Gal. 3:28). If universal and particular identities such as ethnic identities matter in preaching, how should we preach with ethnic and cultural sensitivity?

## Preaching Praxis and the World of Ethnicity and Culture

Some members of the dominant culture may argue that ethnic minorities want to have their cake and eat it too—that is, ethnic minorities want to be considered fully American but want to retain and celebrate their ethnic and cultural backgrounds as well. What do you really want? you ask. The simple answer is that many ethnic minorities want both. Again, we cannot compartmentalize who we are as Americans embodied as persons within a given ethnic group.

If you are from the dominant culture (remember, this can be in any church context where there is a clear majority), put yourself in the shoes of a minority person for a moment. Imagine you are standing around in a circle with others in the church fellowship hall. As a member of the majority culture, you automatically enter the conversation and greet fellow persons in the dominant group with a smile and engage each other amiably in dialogue. However, the minority person, standing silently, may be completely ignored by everyone else in the circle. Hundreds of ticks on the clock go by without any acknowledgment that this person even exists. Eventually, the minority person gets fed up from being snubbed and walks away without any semblance of farewell from those majority persons in the group.

This hypothetical example may seem facetious or exaggerated, but this is the daily reality of most, if not all, minority persons living in America, even in the church. This example has been representative of countless experiences throughout my life both in society and in church life. Minorities are seen but unseen, noticed but unnoticed, acknowledged but unacknowledged, and typically made to feel unwelcome, whether consciously or not. Every week minority congregants in our churches are being ignored. They wander through church life as visible (because they look outwardly different) but invisible (unappreciated and unvalued) beings who enter through the front door and exit silently through the back door. They are often overlooked in normal social interactions and in congregational life, as well as ignored in the proclamation of God's Word.[24]

A preacher who takes the world of ethnicity and culture seriously will intentionally become a student of the different ethnicities and cultures represented in the pews. In the remaining part of this chapter, we will identify ways that we can explore, embrace, and even celebrate the beauty of God's creation in light of ethnicity and culture.

## Practical Steps to Exegete Ethnicity and Culture

Preachers have limited time during their busy weekly schedules. How can a preacher exegete ethnicity and culture with the numerous demands of pastoral life? I would like to suggest some practical steps, given today's time constraints, that will begin to improve one's sermonic reach.

### Personal Study

To begin, we might read existing literature on the topic. In *Counseling American Minorities: A Cross-Cultural Perspective* (McGraw Hill), the authors take the reader on a comprehensive journey to explore the worlds of different racial/ethnic minorities—such as African Americans, Native Americans, Asian Americans, and Hispanic Americans—for the purpose of being able to counsel individuals from these varied backgrounds. Although the book is targeting issues in counseling and not preaching per se, the reader can still enter the world of individuals from these varied cultures in order to better understand how they think and process experiences. Other helpful works related to race, ethnicity, culture, ministry, and homiletics include: *Being White: Finding Our Place in a Multiethnic World* by Paula Harris and Doug Schaupp (InterVarsity); *Preaching to Every Pew: Cross-Cultural Strategies* by James R. Nieman and Thomas G. Rogers (Fortress); *Multicultural Ministry* by David A. Anderson (Zondervan); *Preaching and Culture in Latino Congregations*, edited

---

24. For additional help in considering those who are different from us in our preaching, see Kim, *Preaching with Cultural Intelligence*.

by Kenneth G. Davis and Jorge L. Presmanes (Liturgy Training); *One Gospel, Many Ears* by Joseph R. Jeter Jr. and Ronald J. Allen (Chalice); *I Believe I'll Testify: Reflections on African American Preaching* by Cleophus J. LaRue (Westminster John Knox); and *Preaching the Presence of God: A Homiletic from an Asian American Perspective* by Eunjoo Mary Kim (Judson). I hope my book *Preaching with Cultural Intelligence: Understanding the People Who Hear Our Sermons* (Baker Academic) will be a welcome addition to the mix. As preachers, we are committed to regular study, and this commitment extends to learning about different races, ethnicities, and cultures as well.

### Focus Groups

A second intentional way to learn about different ethnicities and cultures in the congregation is through conducting focus groups. Companies use focus groups regularly as a strategy to discern how best to market their brand and product. Taking a cross section of non-majority individuals from the congregation, the preacher can ascertain how effectively or ineffectively the Sunday sermon is meeting the needs of minority listeners. In most contexts, the preacher will use focus groups to begin exploratory research. Norman Blaikie explains that "exploratory research is necessary when very little is known about the topic being investigated, or about the context in which the research is being conducted."[25]

The preacher could initiate a conversation with members of the congregation who represent different ethnic groups. Similar to the concept of roundtable preaching, advocated by John McClure and Lucy Atkinson Rose,[26] the preacher invites dialogue by asking these congregants the following types of questions:

1. How would you describe yourself in terms of your ethnic identity?
2. In what ways does your ethnicity and culture influence how you listen to and interpret the sermon?
3. Has my preaching ever intersected with your particular ethnic and cultural experience?
4. Have there been any occasions where I have offended, omitted, or misrepresented your ethnicity and culture?
5. How do you think my sermons could improve in tailoring to the experience of non-majority culture members?

25. Norman Blaikie, *Designing Social Research: The Logic of Anticipation* (Cornwall, UK: Polity, 2000), 73.
26. See, e.g., John S. McClure, *The Roundtable Pulpit: Where Leadership and Preaching Meet* (Nashville: Abingdon, 1995); and Lucy Atkinson Rose, *Sharing the Word: Preaching in the Roundtable Church* (Louisville: Westminster John Knox, 1997).

6. Are my sermon applications relevant to your ethnic and cultural context?

7. What do you wish I knew about your ethnicity and culture going forward?

8. How can we as a church celebrate your ethnicity and culture?

Rather than being fearful of how such questions and focus group conversations may be perceived by minority members, know that most non-majority culture parishioners will welcome and appreciate such direct pastoral and homiletical care. Focus groups could become a regular and ongoing part of a preacher's cultural exegesis. Through intentional dialogue, the preacher will gain sermonic insight that may be used intermittently (and wisely) to demonstrate his or her endearment and concern for all members of the flock.

### Friendships and Conversations

Another helpful practice in learning about a specific ethnic group is to establish friendships and engage in informal conversations. As one befriends a person of a different ethnicity and culture, one learns over the course of time that culture differs as well as overlaps. This knowledge shows the homiletician or preacher that we cannot customarily preach a "one-size-fits-all" type of sermon.

The Gospel writers record numerous examples of Jesus befriending others in his life and ministry. He took an active interest in those who were different from himself, those who were considered outcasts in society. Although he could not identify with them on every level (e.g., sin), his many conversations gave him insight into how to meet their individual and collective needs.

A preacher's sole purpose in establishing friendships of this sort should not be to learn about a particular ethnic group only for sermon preparation, and it certainly shouldn't result in people feeling like they have become the pastor's project. However, through genuine shepherd-like care, we can extend our influence both pastorally and sermonically by becoming knowledgeable and sensitive to the God-given differences of others.

### Embrace and Celebrate Ethnicity

As mentioned earlier in this chapter, we may have heard sermons where preachers conclude that the creation of different cultures was God's curse on humanity. Citing Genesis 11 as a primary example, some preachers insist that the Tower of Babel moment was God's pronounced judgment on his people for their sin of self-glorification and that the aftermath resulted in the creation of different languages and ultimately different ethnicities and cultures. If, as

Scripture states, humans are created in the *imago Dei*, is it still plausible that races, ethnicities, and cultures reflect God's curse on certain ethnic groups? Moreover, which ethnicities and cultures constitute God's choice people, and which ethnicities and cultures are cursed? Instead, the judgment of God was directed at the dispersal of his people who felt the need to bring glory to themselves. As Carl F. Keil explains, "When it is stated, first of all, that God resolved to destroy the unity of lips and words by a confusion of the lips, and then that He scattered the men abroad, this act of divine judgment cannot be understood in any other way, than that God deprived them of the ability to comprehend one another, and thus effected their dispersion."[27]

As preachers, we can embrace and celebrate the beauty of God's creation in all ethnicities and cultures. Celebration comes in many forms. One way to celebrate ethnicity is to affirm minority ethnicities within the congregation. Typically, preachers subconsciously paint a picture of only the majority culture as being heroes, heroines, and protagonists. On other occasions, the historic sins, failures, or demise of a particular minority group will be named by the preacher. The unintended consequence of such preaching patterns is that we can demonize minorities and minority groups. Rather, in our illustrations, we can show both groups—majority and minority members—that we indeed value and celebrate minority ethnicities and cultures by offering favorable images of them.[28]

Second, as Nieman and Rogers suggest, celebration of ethnicity may also take the shape of using ethnic words from specific languages that more effectively explain what we are trying to convey. Sometimes we will find that words in other languages like Spanish, Chinese, or German are better suited for the context or situation about which we are speaking. Such words illuminate and illustrate the meaning more poignantly than English words.

Third, celebration of ethnicity could also involve demonstrating to our listeners that we have thought about how the sermon's application might have an impact on one's ethnic group.[29] For example, in Luke 14:26, Jesus tells his disciples: "If anyone comes to me and does not hate father and mother, wife and children, brothers and sisters—yes, even their own life—such a person cannot be my disciple." The application of Jesus's point looks different depending on whether one comes from an individualistic culture or a more collectivistic culture. Individualistic cultures apply God's Word to individual

27. Carl F. Keil, *The Pentateuch: Commentary on the Old Testament*, 2nd ed. (Peabody, MA: Hendrickson, 2006), 110.
28. See Kim, *Preaching with Cultural Intelligence*, chap. 6.
29. See my "Don't Forget about 'Others': Three Ways to Remember 'Others' in Our Sermons," http://www.preachingtoday.com/skills/themes/state-of-preaching/dont-forget-about-others.html.

persons. We turn group instructions in the Bible into personalized instructions for the individual believer. We take what is a "you" plural and repackage it into a "you" singular. In contrast, listeners in collectivistic cultures, such as Asian Americans or Hispanic Americans, where the family unit is more important than the individual, may have more resistance to individualization and want to know how God's Word speaks to the entire community and family, not just the individual. By acknowledging this cultural difference in our sermon, we show listeners from collectivistic backgrounds how to apply this biblical concept in a more contextualized fashion.

Lastly, preaching on ethnicity and culture requires ongoing conversations and active work in reconciliation. In their book *Reconciling All Things*, Emmanuel Katongole and Chris Rice observe, "We live together in a broken world, and we do not have to live long to learn that we need healing. We need reconciliation."[30] The work of reconciliation requires mutual repentance and forgiveness between the offender and the offended.[31] The question we must ask ourselves as preachers is: "When have I [my ethnic group] been the offender and when have I [my ethnic group] been offended?"

The reverberations of the ministry of reconciliation in 2 Corinthians 5:11–21 clearly extend into the domain of ethnic and cultural reconciliation. Remember the ethnic and cultural divisions of the early church between Jews and gentiles? As indicated in Acts 6, human nature is that ethnic groups are self-interested and self-caring. Nobody needed to tell the Jews to care for their own and thereby neglect the Hellenists. The Jews did that instinctively. If we're honest, we do the same today for our own ethnic group even in the same congregation. We feed our own and the rest fend for themselves. We preach to our own and the rest are often forgotten. Preaching in the world of ethnicity and culture invites us to cross cultures. It demands that we repent and seek forgiveness from the offended. How have we perpetuated ethnic divides by our silence? Preaching that embraces and celebrates ethnicity and culture will foster opportunities to break down "the dividing wall of hostility" (Eph. 2:14). When my ethnic group has sinned against another, I must have the humility to ask for forgiveness and repent for my complicity even if I personally did not directly offend the other. It is another form of Paul's proclamation that "I have been crucified with Christ and I no longer live, but Christ lives in me" (Gal. 2:20).

30. Emmanuel Katongole and Chris Rice, *Reconciling All Things: A Christian Vision for Justice, Peace and Healing* (Downers Grove, IL: InterVarsity, 2008), 23.

31. Mark Labberton and Jim Wallis, foreword to *Forgive Us: Confessions of a Compromised Faith*, by Mae Elise Cannon, Lisa Sharon Harper, Troy Jackson, and Soong-Chan Rah (Grand Rapids: Zondervan, 2014), 17.

## Conclusion

Norman A. Hjelm provides a helpful rubric for understanding the relationship between culture and worship, one that can be transferred to preaching as well:

Worship is and should be:

- *Transcultural*: the same substance everywhere, transcending cultures.
- *Contextual*: the transcultural substance expressed locally, adapted from the natural and cultural contexts through the methods of dynamic equivalence or creative assimilation.
- *Countercultural*: challenging and transforming cultural patterns that are inconsistent with the gospel of Jesus Christ.
- *Cross-cultural*: sharing across and between local cultures.[32]

First, preaching is transcultural. The truth of the Bible transcends individual cultures and cultural differences. Second, at the same time, preaching is contextual. Scripture was written from a specific cultural context that speaks into our context. Third, preaching is countercultural, and it challenges cultural sins and deviant cultural values. And yet preaching is also cross-cultural, and this chapter has identified a few of the ways that preaching crosses into different ethnicities and cultures.

In this chapter, I have attempted to put flesh on Haddon Robinson's concept of the worlds of the preacher from a different angle. Specifically, we have been exploring how sermon preparation takes into consideration people of all ethnicities and cultures represented in the church. Our congregations feel the pinch of this ethnic and cultural diversity. They worship next to people who do not look like them, think like them, or act like them. These cultural differences cause us to freeze in each other's presence. While the homiletical norm has been for preachers to generalize sermons with the hope that we will address all listeners, my contention is that our sermonic appeal and influence will expand through intentional study, exploration, and exegesis of varying ethnicities and cultures.

We have merely scratched the surface here. Exegeting the world of ethnicity and culture is a lifelong journey. It will require intentional time, engagement, and sensitivity. It is not a program but rather a lifestyle. We will make mistakes along the way. We may offend congregants unintentionally. We may fall short

32. Norman A. Hjelm, "From the Past to the Future: The LWF Study Series on Worship and Culture as Vision and Mission," in *Worship and Culture: Foreign Country or Homeland?*, ed. Gláucia Vasconcelos Wilkey (Grand Rapids: Eerdmans, 2014), 7.

of loving our neighbors as ourselves. We may not know what questions to ask, or we may ask questions that no one should ask. Yet, through engaging different ethnicities and cultures in our sermons, we are caring for our listeners and demonstrating that they really do matter to us. My hope is that our listeners will feel that pastoral and homiletical care from us more and more each week as we remember the world of ethnicity and culture.

# 6

## The Worlds of the Listener

JEFFREY ARTHURS

## Introduction

Haddon Robinson was passionate about expository preaching, a passion I and the other contributors to this volume share. He conceived of exposition as more than explanation or a verse-by-verse lecture. Rather, it is bridge-building between the worlds of the text and the listeners. As David Larsen states, "A sermon which starts in the Bible and stays in the Bible is not biblical."[1] The metaphor of bridge-building comes from John Stott's *Between Two Worlds*, which Haddon referred to appreciatively in "The Worlds of the Preacher." He also referred to James Cleland's concept of "bi-focal preaching."[2] The preacher must keep an eye on the text and an eye on the congregation, and it is here—contextualizing the ancient Word for modern listeners—that the

1. David Larsen, *The Anatomy of Preaching: Identifying the Issues in Preaching Today* (Grand Rapids: Kregel, 1989), 95.
2. See chap. 1 above. The metaphors are helpful pedagogical tools, conveying much about the theology and art of homiletics, but like all metaphors they obscure even as they illuminate. In particular, they tend to obscure the complexity of communication. They assume a linear model wherein communication flows one way in a straight line so that A says something to B in order to produce an effect. Communication is more complicated than that. "Receivers" are themselves "senders." They do not inertly absorb or resist messages; rather, they collaborate with the communicator to create meaning. Communication is a transaction, a relationship of mutual influence, not the sovereign operation of one agent upon another.

complex, interdisciplinary nature of homiletics shows its colors. Theology, hermeneutics, exegesis, psychology, sociology, rhetoric, and art come into play. C. S. Lewis put it this way: we must "present that which is timeless (the same yesterday, today, and tomorrow) in the particular language of our own age. . . . If you were sent to the Bantus you would be taught their language and traditions. You need similar teaching about the language and mental habits of your own uneducated and unbelieving fellow countrymen."[3] Homileticians in the 1500s made the same point. Puritan William Perkins stated that preachers should expound "the doctrine which has been properly drawn from the Scriptures . . . in ways which are appropriate to the circumstances of the place and time and to the people in the congregation."[4]

This chapter deals with the congregation—the worlds of the listener—for each person and each group has their own culture, language, and history. Specifically, this chapter summarizes and extends one aspect of Robinson's homiletic that helps expositors analyze and adapt to listeners: stage four in Robinson's method, analyzing the exegetical idea with three "developmental questions."[5]

## Probe the Listeners' Responses with Three Developmental Questions

Preachers who desire to stand effectively between two worlds will first articulate the Bible passage's "exegetical idea" (a thorough one-sentence summary of the passage) and then analyze that idea by subjecting it to the following questions (see fig. 1): "What does this mean?" "Is it true?" and "What difference does it make?" When used to probe the text, the questions are a tool of exegesis. They help reveal the author's rhetorical purpose—what he is doing with what he is saying. When used to probe the listeners, the questions are a tool of contextualization, helping the preacher anticipate how the congregation is likely to respond to the passage. The list of developmental questions is a simple heuristic to help expositors anticipate where gaps exist between the ancient text and the modern listeners. To mix my metaphors, the three questions help us speak Bantu.

Robinson's three questions help ministers preach to inspire biblical faith, which requires a response from the whole person, not just mental assent.

---

3. C. S. Lewis, *God in the Dock: Essays on Theology and Ethics* (Grand Rapids: Eerdmans, 1970), 93–94.
4. William Perkins, *The Art of Prophesying* (1592; repr., Carlisle: Banner of Truth, 2011), 54.
5. Haddon W. Robinson, *Biblical Preaching: The Development and Delivery of Expository Messages*, 3rd ed. (Grand Rapids: Baker Academic, 2014), 49–66.

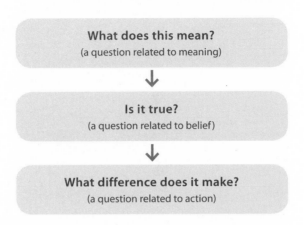

**Figure 1**
**Robinson's Three "Developmental Questions"**

Although I am not aware that Robinson links the three questions to Luther's definition of saving faith (*fides viva*), a parallel can be seen. According to Luther, saving faith is composed of knowledge (*notitia*), which corresponds to Robinson's first question; agreement with the knowledge (*assensus*), which corresponds to the second question; and full-hearted trust in the object of the knowledge (*fiducia*), which corresponds to the third question.

But I'm getting ahead of myself. Before commenting more fully on how the questions function in preaching, let me first illustrate them with everyday communication. You might announce to your spouse, "It's going to rain like crazy tomorrow" (see fig. 2). Your spouse might ask, "What do you mean, 'rain like crazy'?" A gap exists between your "text" (the statement about rain) and your spouse's understanding, so to exposit your "text" you must *explain* the vague statement: "Torrential thunderstorms are coming! It's going to rain two inches between 10 a.m. and 4 p.m. That's what I mean by 'rain like crazy.'" Your spouse says, "Ah! Now I understand." Once that gap is bridged, another may present itself: skepticism. Your spouse seeks proof. He or she asks, "How do you know it's going to 'rain like crazy'?" Your task now is to *convince*, and you might do so by citing the evening news and the weather app on your phone. Both of them warn of torrential thunderstorms. Both of them predict a 100 percent chance that it will "rain like crazy." Your spouse, now convinced, naturally asks: "What should I do? Should I cancel my travel plans?" In this case, you must *apply* the "text," taking the role of advisor or coach.

Notice that the questions are psychologically sequential. Before asking about an idea's validity (the second question), listeners first ask about its meaning

**Figure 2**
## The Developmental Questions and Everyday Conversation
"It's going to rain like crazy tomorrow!"

What do you mean by "rain like crazy"?

How do you know it's going
to "rain like crazy"?

What should I do in light of the fact
that it is going to "rain like crazy"?

**Figure 3**
## The Developmental Questions and Sales
"Buy a whizstick!"

What's a whizstick?
(Listeners usually require at least rudimentary
knowledge before they purchase something,
so to inform them you display the product.)

Why do I need *that*?
(Now that the listeners know what a whizstick is,
persuasion requires that they feel a need for it.)

How can I get one?
(Now that the listeners understand the product and feel
a need for it, they naturally ask how to take action.)

**Figure 4**
## The Developmental Questions and Preaching
*"Avoid sexual immorality."*

> **What's sexual immorality?**
> (To bridge this gap, the preacher serves as teacher/explainer.)

> **What's so bad about sexual immorality?**
> (To bridge this gap, the preacher serves
> as persuader/apologist.)

> **What should I do?**
> (To bridge this gap, the preacher serves as exhorter/coach.)

(the first question). Likewise, listeners do not ask how to take action (the third question) if they do not understand and agree with the statement. Another example illustrates the same dynamic—how customers might respond to a sales talk: "Buy a whizstick!" (see fig. 3).

The three questions help not only spouses and salespeople but also preachers to bridge the gap. Let's say that the preacher is speaking on 1 Thessalonians 4:1–8 at a high school retreat. The exegetical idea is "Live to please God by avoiding sexual immorality." While preparing the sermon, the preacher uses Robinson's three questions to identify the listeners' responses—the gaps that are likely to be present (see fig. 4).

The preacher listens to the exegetical idea through the ears of the high school students. The first question—"What does this mean?"—is pertinent because the students are confused not about sex but about "immorality." They have a general notion that married people should not have sex with someone who is not their spouse, but the students wonder about sex between unmarried people. Is that "immorality"? And what about nonintercourse sex? Does the idea include that? How about pornography? Relevant exposition requires the preacher to assume the role of teacher, patiently and clearly explaining the idea. The minister might explain that the phrase "sexual immorality" is a translation of the Greek word *porneia*, a general word for all kinds of sexual misconduct, not just adultery. The preacher might illustrate *porneia* with examples from movies and current events. Of course, choosing illustrations will demand wisdom so that the preacher will edify, not inflame, the students.

After the gap of knowledge is narrowed, the preacher is not home yet, since the Holy Spirit wants the listeners to *avoid* sexual immorality, not just understand it. As the preacher seeks to enact the author's rhetorical purpose, he or she may encounter a second gap—one of belief. The students now *understand* the command from God, but they are *skeptical* about its validity, just as a spouse may be skeptical about the forecast or a customer may be skeptical about the value of a whizstick.

Why might the students be skeptical? Numerous reasons come to mind, but two stand out: the influences of media and peers. These are the highest authorities for many young people when they emerge from the canopy of their parents' beliefs. Movies, television, music, the internet, friends, classmates, and teammates often drum a metronomic cadence of worldliness, discipling the students that the lust of the flesh, the lust of the eyes, and the pride that comes from owning and displaying things is normal and good. Media and peers are the de facto authorities for many young people (and old people!), forming their beliefs and values, hardening their hearts. The Word is sown— "avoid sexual immorality"—but it falls on hard ground and the devil snatches it away. Or it sprouts but is soon choked by life's worries, riches, and pleasures (Luke 8:1–14). As the daughter of a friend recently said when she and her mother talked about sexual immorality, "Mom, things are different now." She meant that the old standards no longer apply. The daughter still believes in "God and Jesus and the Bible and stuff," but all of that must conform to the modern values displayed in media and expressed by peers. When ministering to young people, exposition of the 1 Thessalonians passage demands that the preacher go beyond explanation into persuasion. J. I. Packer echoes this conviction: preaching is a "kind of speaking aimed at both mind and heart, and seeking unashamedly to change the way people think and live. So it is always an attempt at persuasion."[6]

Preaching that overcomes skepticism addresses the heart. In the Bible, the "heart" is an amalgamation of ideas, beliefs, values, feelings, and memories (see fig. 5). It is the interior motivational structure that produces behavior. In the case of the high school retreat, it is likely that the students are not fully aware of why they are skeptical about the 1 Thessalonians passage; nevertheless, media and peers are the hidden gatekeepers of their hearts.

Only the Holy Spirit can change the heart, yet the Spirit chooses regularly to use the preaching of the Word to save and sanctify. The Word is water that

6. J. I. Packer, cited in Wallace Benn, "Preaching with a Pastor's Heart: Richard Baxter's *The Reformed Pastor*," in *Preach the Word*, ed. Leland Ryken and Todd Wilson (Wheaton: Crossway, 2007), 137.

**Figure 5**
**Biblical View of the "Heart"**

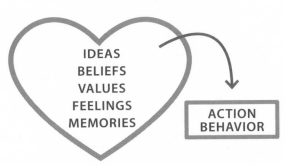

IDEAS
BELIEFS
VALUES
FEELINGS
MEMORIES

ACTION
BEHAVIOR

cleanses, milk that nourishes, a sword that pierces, a lamp for guidance, fire that purifies, seed that grows and bears fruit, a mirror that shows us our true selves, and a hammer that breaks stone (Eph. 5:26; Heb. 5:12–14; 4:12; Ps. 119:105; Jer. 23:29; 1 Pet. 1:23; James 1:23–25). So the preacher must present the Word—"avoid sexual immorality"—in a way that is not only understandable (Robinson's first question) but also persuasive (his second question).

To do this, the preacher must fully comprehend and empathize with the listeners' skepticism. He or she must be able to articulate the students' doubts accurately and compassionately. As Robinson says, failing to consider the listeners' heartfelt questions "means we will speak only to those who are already committed. . . . A congregation has the right to expect that we are at least aware of the problems before we offer solutions."[7] Although Robinson doesn't use the term "identification" from rhetorician Kenneth Burke,[8] he seems to have it in mind with statements like this: "I do everything I can to show people that I respect them and I'm on their side."[9] Only when the preacher identifies with the listeners will the gatekeepers stand aside.

When preaching from the 1 Thessalonians passage, the minister might identify with the young people by unashamedly pointing out that God made sex as a pleasurable and bonding experience, thus affirming, in part, the "authorities" the youth look up to. The preacher might also use facts and

7. Robinson, *Biblical Preaching*, 57.
8. Burke comments on "identification": "You persuade a man only insofar as you can talk his language by speech, gesture, tonality, order, image, attitude, idea, identifying your ways with his. . . . True, the rhetorician may have to change the audience's opinion in one respect; but he can succeed only insofar as he yields to that audience's opinions in other respects." Kenneth Burke, *A Rhetoric of Motives* (Berkeley: University of California Press, 1950), 55–56.
9. Haddon W. Robinson, *Making a Difference in Preaching*, ed. Scott M. Gibson (Grand Rapids: Baker, 1999), 125.

quotations from research to show that the highest levels of sexual satisfaction are reported by married, monogamous couples as they experience sex within the bonds of covenantal love. To counter the notion that "things are different now," the preacher could show the young people that this teaching on *porneia* is consistent through the whole Bible and church history, spanning thousands of years and extending to the present time. And effective persuasion will not neglect to warn the students, as 1 Thessalonians 4:6 does, that the Lord punishes believers who take advantage of others.

While a single twenty-five-minute message is unlikely to overturn thousands of hours of "preaching" from media and peers, a steady, patient, clear, and skillful ministry of the Word can result in salvation and sanctification when the Spirit gives ears to hear.

The third question—"What difference does this make?"—builds on the expositor's work as a teacher and persuader. It calls the minister to also serve as an exhorter, advisor, and mentor. Preachers can take heart as they assume these roles, because listeners crave practical application.[10]

Robinson explains the third question: "When I understand an eternal truth or guiding principle, what specific, practical applications does this have for me and my congregation? What ideas, feelings, attitudes, or actions should it affect? Do I myself live in obedience to this truth? . . . What obstacles keep my audience from responding as they should? What suggestions might help them respond as God wants them to respond?"[11] Preachers make disciples by teaching listeners to *obey* all things our Lord taught. Action is the telos of all biblical teaching because it is the telos of the Bible itself. Biblical scholar Bernard Ramm put it this way: "Holy Scripture is not a theoretical book of theological abstraction, but a book that intends to have a mighty influence on the lives of its readers."[12]

Going back to our example from 1 Thessalonians, the preacher might coach the students to "avoid sexual immorality" with this concrete advice:

> Learn to control your body in holiness and honor as verse 4 teaches. Develop standards and safeguards before you find yourself in temptation. For example, do you have standards about what movies you will and will not watch, or do you just watch whatever is available? I heard about a fellow who goes to the theater without even knowing what is playing. He just shows up and chooses

10. One study that shows this is Lori Carrell's *The Great American Sermon Survey* (Wheaton: Mainstay Church Resources, 2000), 88–89, 113–14.

11. Robinson, *Biblical Preaching*, 92.

12. Bernard Ramm, *Protestant Biblical Interpretation*, 3rd ed. (Grand Rapids: Baker, 1985), 113.

something that starts in a few minutes. That "standard" is going to let him down if he hopes to obey this verse: "Avoid sexual immorality." Instead of bumbling along naively in this culture of hypersexuality, try doing a little research before you go to the movies. I use the website called kids-in-mind.com. It describes in detail why each movie has received its rating. After reading that website, I'm in a much better place to consider if the movie will help me "avoid sexual immorality."

In summary, Robinson's list of questions is a simple and effective way to think through how a text intersects with the listeners' knowledge, agreement, and behavior. But the question naturally arises: How can a preacher know what is in the hearts of the listeners—how are we to assess their level of knowledge and assent? This is an important question and deserves more discussion in homiletical literature than it receives. It is the question of "audience analysis." If exposition is indeed bridge-building, then the preacher needs to exegete the congregation and not just the text, but that is not easy to do. One difficulty is that a congregation is made up of individuals. Perfect knowledge of one listener (which is itself unattainable) is no guarantee of accurate knowledge of the person seated to her right. The high school retreat has students ranging in their Christian maturity from seeker to fully devoted. The group undoubtedly has some young people with a high degree of knowledge and some with a low degree. The same is true regarding each person's level of agreement with the text's main idea. What's a preacher to do? We can't look into hearts, and even if we could, every heart is unique.

## How Can the Preacher Enter the Worlds of the Listeners?

Five tools help preachers exegete the listeners. These tools may seem mechanical or wooden to experienced pastors who have intuitive knowledge of their listeners. After all, they marry, bury, baptize, and counsel, so they already have a good deal of insight into the flock. Nevertheless, even experienced pastors can benefit from an intentional approach to "congregational exegesis."

### Tool One: You

First, start with yourself. While preparing the sermon, use the three questions to monitor your own reactions to the text. Identify where gaps exist. While your reactions to the text will not be identical to the listeners', some of your responses will overlap with theirs. First Thessalonians 4:6 says, "The Lord will punish all those who commit such sins" (NIV) or "the Lord is an avenger in all these things" (ESV). Do you know what this means? Do you believe it? Start with yourself, and you will identify some of the questions that are likely to niggle in the hearts and minds of the youth group.

Starting with yourself provides another benefit: credibility. Modern listeners rightly crave authenticity, so we must ask ourselves: Am I living the kind of life I am recommending to others? When the sermon first percolates through the personality and experience of the preacher, it has the ring of authenticity.

### Tool Two: Your Listeners

The second tool for congregational exegesis is spending informal time with them. The majority of a pastor's interactions with the flock occur at formal functions of the church, so we are wise to interact with parishioners at other times as well. It is one thing to spend time together at a Sunday service, board meeting, or prayer meetings; it is another thing to play softball together, paint a shed, or visit parishioners at work and home. Home visitation is dwindling in many church cultures, but a lot of "audience analysis" can be done in one hour spent in the living room of a church member.

Similarly, many pastors are helped by spending time interacting in the broader community. Government publications on community demographics provide specifics about the people in your community, and simply driving around with eyes open (a recommended practice any time you drive!) yields much information. Who is moving in and out? How are the businesses doing on Main Street?

David Ridder set out to discover if our culture still has a sense of sin, and he conducted some of his "research" simply by conversing with people at a local coffee shop.[13] I'll return to Ridder's work below, but here the point is: spend time with people. Do so as a "soul-watcher" (Heb. 13:17), a term that reminds us that we observe, protect, and tend souls.

### Tool Three: Counseling

A third tool is counseling. The roles of counselor and preacher support each other. Speaking as both a counselor and homiletician, Jay Adams observes that counselors benefit from doing regular exegesis for sermon preparation, and likewise preachers benefit from time spent in the counselor's chamber. When a preacher spends more time with commentaries than with people,

---

13. David A. Ridder, "The Application of Missionary Elenctics to Preaching to Postmoderns" (unpublished paper presented at the Evangelical Homiletics Society, 2008).

he or she sounds like a book in the pulpit.[14] While the preacher should never reveal someone else's personal material in the pulpit, the preacher who is also a counselor—in other words, a *pastor*—will note trends and patterns in the congregation. For example, in one church where I served, the elders of the church compared notes on who they were currently counseling, and we discovered that nine couples in our small church were experiencing marital stress. We saw that Satan was attacking our church in this area, and we met the challenge by increasing our prayer and by preaching and teaching on marriage.

### Tool Four: Feedforward

The three tools above are informal means of discovering where gaps exist, but the fourth is formal: gain "feedforward." Feedforward is similar to feedback, but the communicator seeks information and reaction *before* speaking rather than after. We do not want to preach in the dark. Here is a list of ways preachers can seek feedforward:

- Use a suggestion box to allow listeners to ask questions and give input.
- Use an application grid (see fig. 6). List categories that help you exegete the listeners.
- Conduct your own survey. In the seminary where I teach, the faculty preached a series in chapel entitled "Doubt." As dean of the chapel, I sent a very brief anonymous survey to the entire student body with these questions: (1) What causes you to doubt? and (2) What do you do when you doubt? I cataloged the responses I received and then shared them with the preachers for the series. The feedforward helped them serve as soul-watchers.
- Conduct a professional survey. This can be expensive, but I have found it to be very beneficial. Consulting groups like Vital Church (www.vital churchministry.org) can discover and summarize information such as church demographics, level of awareness and enthusiasm for the church's mission, and what motivates folks to attend. One church where I served used a survey created by Willow Creek Community Church to discover where attenders were on their spiritual journey.[15] This church was located in a college town, and we intentionally reached out to students.

14. Jay E. Adams, *Preaching with Purpose: The Urgent Task of Homiletics* (Grand Rapids: Zondervan, 1982), 38.

15. See http://revealforchurch.com. The survey was based on eighty thousand people in two hundred congregations. The follow-up study, called *Follow Me*, by Greg L. Hawkins and

## Figure 6
## Application Grid

*"For he himself is our peace, who has made us both one and has broken
down in his flesh the dividing wall of hostility" (Eph. 2:14).*

**How would individuals respond to that verse?
What questions might they ask?**

| Age | Gender | Marital Status | Occupation | Health | Spiritual State |
|---|---|---|---|---|---|
| Pre-teen | | | | | |
| Teen | Female | Single | Student, part-time babysitting | Broken wrist | Maturing Christian, conflict with . . . |
| 20s | Male | Single | Bus driver | Good | Young Christian, inconsistent with spiritual disciplines |
| 40s | Female | Single (divorced) | Administrator in public school | Fair, concerned about being overweight | Growing Christian, serves in the church and the community, part of an accountability group, has questions about the roles of women in the church |
| 70s | Male | Single | Retired military | Fair, high blood pressure | Immature, shows signs of prejudice |
| Etc. | | | | | |

While I knew the mission and strategy of the church, I was still surprised to learn that more than 50 percent of the folks listening to my preaching described themselves as either seekers or young in the faith. When I discovered that, my preaching changed. I started dealing with fewer concepts, spending more time on each concept. Haddon Robinson often said that "less is more." Fewer concepts addressed in more detail results in greater impact. I could not assume that just because a truth was found in the Bible that the listeners automatically assented to it, so I used more proof and illustration to expound the Scriptures. To be sure, the students were not antagonistic toward the faith, but neither were they mature Christians who had settled basic issues of their beliefs.

Cally Parkinson (n.p.: Willow Creek Association, 2008), describes the spiritual practices that help people grow in Christ.

### Tool Five: Pay Attention to Cultural Trends

A fifth tool of congregational analysis is simply paying attention to cultural trends as revealed in media. Timothy Keller keeps up a rigorous habit of reading, deliberately perusing periodicals that range from conservative to radical, to understand the values, lifestyles, and worldviews of his highly secularized and skeptical congregation in New York City. Worldview is often revealed and extended through movies, music, advertising, and television. That's where the spirit of the age blows. Secular answers to the questions each worldview seeks to answer are embedded in our entertainment media—"Who am I?" "Why am I on earth?" "What is wrong with the world?" and "How can we make things right?"

Take that third question—"What is wrong with the world?" In the North American context, answers will include politics, racism, poor education, and religions that breed intolerance. A biblical worldview sees all of those connected directly or indirectly to sin, but few people today feel a sense of personal responsibility for violating God's laws. Or do they? Carefully listening to media reveals that people still experience conviction in ways that are congruent with the Bible's definitions of sin. This is where David Ridder's research comes in. He tapped into the field of study called "missionary elenctics" to argue that North American pastors, not just overseas missionaries, should contextualize their message.[16] A person engaging in elenctics observes a culture to discover and display where conviction is already present in people's consciences, so that preachers can "speak of moral failure in terms the conscience will ratify in a given cultural context."[17]

One of the best ways to do elenctics is by viewing media to see how artists "define" moral failure. Most people are too defensive to admit their own sins, but by observing where they express disgust and outrage at other people's sins, we can see the standards of conscience they operate with. By viewing art, such as films, where the viewer "judges" the characters on the screen, elenctics reveals a culture's standards of right and wrong.

For example, at the time Ridder did his research, the popularity of superhero movies was taking off (and as I write this chapter in 2017, that popularity is still on the rise). In those fantasies we see an elenctic theme: power. Postmodern artists regularly call viewers to use power for good, but they also recognize

16. The word "elenctics" comes from the Greek word *elenchō*, "to bring to light, expose." This is the word used in John 16:8—the Holy Spirit "will prove the world to be in the wrong about sin." Romans 2:14–16, which speaks about conscience, is another key passage in forming a theology of the Spirit's work of conviction.

17. Ridder, "Missionary Elenctics," 1.

that power uses us. Batman's dark motives in battling the Joker separate him only by an inch from his twisted archfoe. Iron Man's use of technological brilliance is a tool for self-gratification. Power has a dark side. In *Harry Potter and the Half-Blood Prince*, Harry Potter discovers a dusty book that contains shortcuts for some difficult magical arts. Hermione warns him to set the book aside because they don't know who it belonged to, but Harry enjoys how it helps him breeze through his charms class without studying. Then he comes upon his enemy, Draco Malfoy. They get into a fight and Harry uses one of the curses in the book like a sword to slash Draco's face. Harry has power, but something within causes him to use the power destructively. As the uncle of Peter Parker (Spider-Man) states: "With great power comes great responsibility," and postmoderns are aware that they sometimes fail to use their power responsibly.

## How to Bridge the Gap?

Having laid out Robinson's heuristic set of three questions and having suggested some ways to exegete the listeners, the final issue this chapter examines

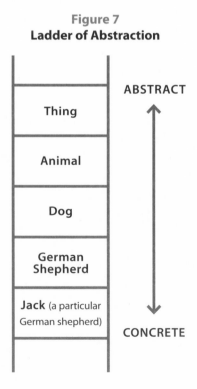

**Figure 7**
**Ladder of Abstraction**

**Figure 8**
**Three Operations of the Mind**

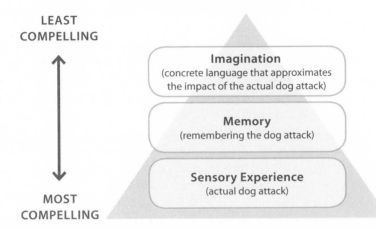

is how to bridge the gap—how to explain, prove, and apply. We do so with concrete support material such as story, examples, analogy, self-disclosure, and metaphor. The key word in that sentence is "concrete." The human mind forms no image of an abstract, vague term. Thus communication that is heavy on abstraction rivets little attention, clarifies few ideas, and stirs no emotion. Effective communicators spend much of their time on the lower rungs of the ladder of abstraction (see fig. 7).

The power of concrete language has been recognized for millennia. Classical rhetoric spoke often of *enargeia* (Greek) and *visiones* (Latin). These mean the use of vivid language that brings images before the mind's eye. Rather than saying, "Going to war with Sparta will result in dire consequences for Athens," the ancient rhetoricians might recommend saying, "If you go to war with Sparta, your men will bleed, your women will wail, your navies will sink, and your city will burn."

While classical rhetoric recognized the efficacy of concrete language, not until the 1800s did rhetorical theory offer an explanation for why it is more persuasive than dull language. That explanation came in the work of Scottish clergyman and philosopher George Campbell.[18] Using nineteenth-century discoveries in the "brain science" of his day, he propounded three "operations of the mind" that determine three levels of belief (see fig. 8).[19] The most

18. George Campbell, *Philosophy of Rhetoric*, ed. Lloyd Bitzer (Carbondale: Southern Illinois University Press, 1988).

19. Although he was writing in the early 1800s, Campbell's work was prescient. Modern neuroscience has verified it, at least in terms of visual imagery. Concrete language activates the

convincing operation is *sensory experience*, such as the experience of being attacked by a dog. While the attack is occurring, it captures your full attention and provides all the "proof" necessary to convince you that the snapping dog is real and dangerous. The second operation is *memory*. At times, simply remembering something (such as the time when you were attacked by a dog) can hold attention, stir emotion, and compel belief as effectually as actual experience. Third is *imagination*. Even when a listener has not been attacked by a dog, persuaders can still move him or her by using language that sparks imagination.[20] To do so requires the use of concrete language—images.

Preachers rarely use the first operation of the mind—actual sensory experience—although there is a growing and welcome trend toward multi-sensory preaching.[21] Sermonizing is primarily a verbal act. Preachers sometimes use the second operation of the mind by evoking memory of actual experience, such as a time when God answered prayer. In this way we help listeners obey the Bible's oft-repeated commands: "remember" (Deut. 5:15; 7:18; Ps. 105:5) and "do not forget" (Heb. 13:16; 2 Pet. 3:8).[22] But preachers mostly use the third operation. Oral discourse normally explains, proves, and applies truth by utilizing imagination. Robinson illustrates this principle:

> If I say, "Irritation bothers us all," I'm speaking to no one in particular. . . . We do better to focus specifically on two or three types of people. . . . I might illustrate a sermon on conflict by saying, "You live with your roommate, and your roommate has some irritating habits, like not cleaning the dishes right after the meal. Or you're married, and your husband comes home and plops himself in front of the TV without any regard for what your day has been like."[23]

---

same areas of the brain and uses the same neural pathways as actual visual experience. Thus, in the brain, concrete language gets attention, compels belief, and stirs emotion in ways similar to actual sight. This helps explain the rhetorical power of orations rich with metaphor and image such as Martin Luther King Jr.'s "I Have a Dream" and Jonathan Edwards's "Sinners in the Hands of an Angry God." Listeners were caught up in imaginative experience as the orators used concrete language. See, e.g., G. Lupyan, S. L. Thompson-Schill, and D. Swingley, "Conceptual Penetration of Visual Processing," *Psychological Science* 21 (2010): 682–91; and G. Lupyan and E. J. Ward, "Language Can Boost Otherwise Unseen Objects into Visual Awareness," *Proceedings of the National Academy of Sciences* 110 (2013): 14196–201.

20. As early as the 1600s, Francis Bacon defined "rhetoric" as "the application of *Reason to Imagination* for the better moving of the will." Francis Bacon, *Selected Writings of Francis Bacon*, ed. Hugh C. Dick (New York: Modern Library, 1955), x.

21. Furthermore, in the context of a worship service, preaching works in tandem with ceremony and ritual (actual sensory experience).

22. See Jeffrey D. Arthurs, *Preaching as Reminding: How to Stir Memory in an Age of Forgetfulness* (Downers Grove, IL: InterVarsity, 2017).

23. Robinson, *Making a Difference in Preaching*, 121.

Return to the example of the high school retreat and the sermon from 1 Thessalonians—"avoid sexual immorality." The word "avoid" could be explained with an object lesson that employs sensory experience: you could throw a ball at a member of the youth group and have him or her dodge it. The object lesson functions as an analogy: avoiding sexual immorality is like dodging the ball. Or you could illustrate the command by using memory, recounting the testimony the youth group heard last year from a young man who learned how to avoid pornography. Both of those tools can rivet attention and prompt belief, but the most common tool preaching uses is "mere" discourse—exposition, argumentation, and illustration. The discourse must be concrete so that it approximates the power of experience or memory. Listeners do not want to be marooned on the shores of abstraction.

Perhaps it would be helpful if I came down the ladder of abstraction myself with an example from Robinson's own preaching. He was speaking in a seminary chapel on Matthew 25: "Whatever you did for one of the least of these brothers and sisters of mine, you did for me" (v. 40).[24] All of the students knew that verse, and I imagine some of them had even preached it, so Robinson's job was not to explain or prove a new truth but to apply an old truth. He sought to move them to respond. Here is a close paraphrase:

> Since it's the judgment of the nations, I imagine I'll be there. I'll be standing before the King and he'll say, "Robinson, did you bring your datebook? Look up October 27, 28, 29, 1983."
>
> "Oh yes, Lord. That's when I was made president of the Evangelical Theological Society. We had a big meeting down in Dallas. I wrote a paper: 'The Relationship of Hermeneutics to Homiletics.'"
>
> And the King will say, "Well, I don't know anything about that. I don't go to many of those meetings. No, what I had in mind happened before you went to Dallas. There was a married couple on your campus. I allowed them to have a twenty-five-day check in a thirty-one-day month. Bonnie told you about them. And you folks put some money in an envelope and put it in their box. Remember that?"
>
> "Wow, that was so long ago. Bonnie would probably remember it better than I would."
>
> But the King will say, "I remember it. You put that money in that box and gave it to me. I've never forgotten it. Look at the first week in March of 1994."
>
> "Oh yes, Lord, that's when I was mentioned in *Newsweek* magazine as one of the best religious communicators in the English-speaking world!"

24. Haddon W. Robinson, "The Sheep and the Goats," audio recording of a sermon preached at Gordon-Conwell Theological Seminary, South Hamilton, MA, March 2011.

"Well, I don't read those magazines much. They're so inaccurate. No, I was thinking of when you were teaching on that day. You were leaving class to go to a meeting, and there was a young woman sitting there, and you said, 'How are you doing?' She began to weep. You sat down and she told you that her brother had passed away a couple of days ago and her father a couple of months ago. She found the burden of that grief so heavy that she didn't know if she could bear it. And you didn't know what to say, so you just listened. Remember that?"

"Yeah, I guess I do. I felt so inadequate."

And the King will say, "When you stopped to listen to that woman, you were listening to me, and I have never forgotten it."

There are going to be a lot of surprises at the judgment. You know all that stuff you put on your résumé? It won't matter much. What will matter will be acts of kindness and compassion.

## Conclusion

The old adage "Those who can't do, teach" does not apply to Haddon Robinson. The quality of his preaching matched the insight of his instruction. He analyzed his listeners to see where gaps existed between the congregation and the text, thinking through the questions they might ask: "What does this mean?" "Is it true?" and "What difference does it make?" And he responded to those questions with vivid, powerful language. Through precept and example, Robinson blessed the church by equipping ministers to be capable expositors.

# 7

## Preaching in This Present World

PATRICIA M. BATTEN

### Introduction

I worked with Haddon Robinson for the five years just prior to his retirement. I still picture his routine. He went to the gym, ate breakfast in the cafeteria (declining donuts and muffins), and spent some time in his corner office before taking the elevator (if his knee hadn't bothered him, he would have opted for the stairs) down one level to AC 254. He arrived a minute or two before 8 a.m. He was never frazzled. Not once. Every morning when he walked in the classroom I smiled and said, "Good morning, Haddon!" His reply was always the same: "What's so good about it?"

Every so often, he walked into the room with a manila file folder in hand that contained one or two transparencies for the overhead projector. One lecture required a prop. But like Haddon's sermons, his lectures were stored in his head. In fact, the word "lecture" doesn't fit what he did. Like his preaching, his teaching was more conversational.

One morning I asked him if I could update the few transparencies he had by putting them on PowerPoint. He responded with a cautious "Yes." He preferred limited use of handouts and words on a screen because it might detract from the eye contact he had with the listeners.

Most lectures didn't make use of visual aids at all, except for the lecture called "The Worlds of the Preacher." He wanted a picture for each of the four worlds: ancient, modern, particular church, personal. For the ancient world, I inserted a picture of Moses with the stone tablets. The modern world showed a globe with a computer and other electronic devices. The particular church world revealed a church that might be found anywhere in America. The personal world was a close-up of a young woman wearing black-rimmed glasses, smiling a toothy grin.

In this chapter we'll zoom in on the world of the preacher's listeners: the preacher's particular church world. Not any church. Your church. The one with a street address and zip code.

Your particular church has a history, a language, and a culture. Both preachers and parishioners are well served when an understanding, evaluation, appreciation, and participation in the world of the local congregation is a pastoral priority. Why? Because it's connected to preaching. Understanding one's particular church context makes a difference in the pulpit. How does knowing the particular world of your church affect your preaching?

Let's begin with history. Your church's history may help you understand your listeners better so that you can connect with them more.

## Appreciate the History of Your Ministry Setting

In 1775, Thomas Ditson saddled his horse and rode twenty-five miles into Boston from Billerica, Massachusetts. He wanted to purchase a musket. Instead, he was captured by British forces. He was tarred, feathered, and paraded through the streets of Boston while soldiers mocked him with a song:

> Yankee Doodle came to town,
> For to buy a firelock,
> We will tar and feather him,
> And so we will John Hancock.

As the story of Ditson's public humiliation spread, that Yankee Doodle ditty became a battle cry for minutemen across the region. The simple rhyming verse rallied farmers and blacksmiths and bellfounders to take up arms and fight. And even the pain of tar-induced blisters did not deter Ditson from battle. One month after the incident, Ditson fought at the Battle of Meriam's Corner in Concord.[1]

Today, every child in Billerica, Massachusetts, grows up hearing Ditson's story. His spirit of Yankee pride, endurance, and grit still mark the people of this town. And those are good qualities. They're also qualities that a preacher

---

1. Rick Sobey, "Just Dandy, Patriots! Billerica's the 'Yankee Doodle Town,'" *Lowell Sun*, September 28, 2016, http://www.lowellsun.com/breakingnews/ci_30409856/just-dandy -patriots-billericas-yankee-doodle-town#ixzz4VZ9pIwvt.

can tap into and redeem. Endurance can easily become a source of selfish pride, but enduring with the knowledge that a good and gracious God upholds you is a posture of humility. Preachers can launch a perspective shift from the pulpit by reminding parishioners to lift up their eyes to the God who always watches over them and helps them. Preachers would do well to examine the history that informs the culture and shine the light of Christ on it.

When that history is good and noble and glorifying to God, it can be tapped into to spur on the congregation and remind them of who they were and who they are now.

I remember shuffling through a box of old papers at my little church in Kennebunkport, Maine. I came across a proclamation from the governor, dated 1850. It was a call for the people to go to their places of worship and urgently call on God. The issue was one of great consequence. It had to do with the Fugitive Slave Act. Prior to 1850, slaves could not be chased once they were in the free states. Maine was a free state. But then came the Fugitive Slave Act, which made it illegal to help escaped slaves. Bounty hunters were allowed to go into free states and capture runaways. Anyone who aided an escaped slave would be punished and fined. Many say that this act played a major role in forcing the nation closer to civil war. So, on the brink of war, Mainers—people in all the free states, in fact—assembled to seek God.

The first paragraph of the proclamation read: "It is the duty of a dependent people to remember their obligations." At the outset, people knew that they were dependent on God. Reading further: "of a sinful people to confess their unworthiness." They knew that they were dependent on God and that they were sinful—and unworthy of God's grace. "A penitent people"—meaning sorrowful for their sin—seeking God's forgiveness.

A day was set for fasting, humiliation, and prayer: Thursday, April 10, 1851—no work, no play. Just church. The middle of the paragraph: "And let not the day that is set apart for the special discharge of these solemn duties, be made a day of idle dissipation, or of frivolous amusements." It was to be taken seriously so that God "would of His great mercy pardon all our sins, granting us that true repentance which shall be unto reformation of life."

One hundred fifty years before I came to that church, the very first pastor, Reverend Nott, led the congregation as they met corporately for fasting, prayer, and humiliation. Our nation was divided and on the brink of war. They needed to turn to God.

Remembering how a church responded to challenges in the past can help us see how we might proceed in present predicaments. We need to turn to God.

Appreciate the history of your church. That doesn't mean that every aspect of the history of your local congregation is worthy of praise, but when you know the history, you can evaluate it. Then you'll understand why your parishioners think or speak or act the way they do. You can meet the need through your preaching.

## Appreciate the Culture of Your Local Congregation

Haddon Robinson preached at my church in Kennebunkport three times. The last time he preached, I made dinner reservations for him and Bonnie at an oceanside restaurant not far from Walker's Point, the summer residence of former president George H. W. Bush.

When I saw Haddon the next morning, he greeted me with a smile and said, "You'll never guess who was at the table next to us last night."

Of course, I knew that George and Barbara Bush often ate at the inn near their seaside home. Haddon got a kick out of it, and in the process he experienced a beloved piece of Kennebunkport culture: a former president and first lady. Yes, politics and pedigree were part of the fabric of Kennebunkport, but it wasn't everything. If Haddon walked away thinking, "This is Kennebunkport," he would have had only a fraction of the story, and he would have missed the colorful, character-driven, commonsense culture of my congregation that tasted more like homemade apple pie than a five-course meal, that sounded more like a country song than a symphony.

The parishioners of my church were more likely to eat "supper" than "dinner." Most preferred to trek inland to the Maine Diner and wait in a long line of chattering patrons than reserve a wait-less seat at an inn at the edge of the sea. They were a ham-and-beans kind of people. Moose-meat pie. Boiled dinners and stuffed cabbage rolls. Lobster stew. Venison from the basement freezer. Deals were forged with a handshake, not a pen. Love was expressed in the concrete: "Borrow my truck" or "I'll watch the kids." Sixty years married and still holding hands while moseying down the lane at the town fair; handwritten notes and handmade crafts. Bake from scratch and give the shirt off your back. (Can you hear the country song starting to form?)

My church had a culture of its own. Appreciate your church's culture. Don't look down on it. Don't try to convert a country song into a symphony or swap out apple pie for crème brûlée.

## Don't Trash the Dump Parade

About a year into my first pastorate, a woman in her late thirties sat across from me in the pastor's study. I'm sure the look on my face gave me away. "You hold the *Miss Dumpy* title?" I asked. "*What on earth is that?*"

For years, our community held a "Dump Parade." Floats filled with refuse filed down the streets. Garlands of dead fish ornamented pickup trucks. Men and women draped shawls made from bottles and capes from cans over their shoulders. A basket of rotten fruit adorned the head of a young lady. It was the annual Dump Parade. At the end of it all, Miss Dumpy was crowned queen of the landfill.

The Dump Parade was a unique part of Kennebunkport culture. It began in 1965 as a way to create environmental awareness. The Dump Association wanted more trash in the landfill and less on the streets. The parade served to promote the dump. And let's face it, the town dump was a terrific Saturday morning meeting place—a setting for camaraderie and connection.

We can appreciate the culture in our ministry setting from the pulpit. What does that actually look and sound like from the pulpit? You don't need to sew a suit of trash or wear an old sandwich on your head as you preach, but pay attention to what's going on outside the walls of your church. If it's the Sunday after the Dump Parade, perhaps you might preach on a passage that deals with caring for God's creation—Genesis 1 or 2 or Psalm 24, in which the psalmist reminds us that "the earth is the LORD's, and everything in it" (v. 1). Use illustrations that your congregation can relate to and that are relevant to their lives. Speak positively about the good things in their culture—that is, *don't trash the Dump Parade.*

I have a friend who refused to attend a church because the preacher wore a suit and the congregation dressed in their Sunday best. I take it his problem wasn't really with the clothing but with the culture. The jacket attire represented a formal culture of worship rather than a familial one. I think if I pressed him he might admit that he thought a church of dresses and suits smacked of inauthenticity. Like kids in a costume closet, he viewed it as dress-up worship. Play. Pretend.

But the goal isn't to get those who wear suits to wear denim or those who wear denim to wear suits. Some people are more at home in a button-down sweater than in sweatpants. They're more comfortable in dress pants than in denim. Don't look down on the culture. Don't trash the dump. Don't force denim on dress pants. Appreciate the culture of your congregation. When we do, we're connecting with our listeners. But even more than connecting, we're loving them. Taking an interest in the things that are important to others is a good way to express love.

## Evaluate to Elevate

Not everything in our local congregation should be appreciated from the pulpit. I remember my first board meeting that involved yelling. We were talking about singing a praise song with the kids when suddenly a fist smacked the table and an angry voice thundered, "Over my dead body!" We had struck a minor chord in a major way. Part of me wanted to laugh and say, "Did you really just shout that out? Did you really hit the table? How do we move forward from 'dead body'? It's so *extreme*." I shouldn't have been surprised. This particular person was skilled at the "shock effect." She created a culture of fear. Others were afraid to voice their opinions.

Evaluate church language and culture to determine if it needs elevating. What is the culture of the church environment? We hear a lot about "workplace culture," but what is "churchplace culture"? This is a world that the preacher must know and must address when it needs attention.

What's the invisible character and personality of the church? What are the attitudes of key leaders and worker bees? How do people talk to one another? Are they gracious in their language or condemning? Are comments snarky and conversations superficial? Or are words filled with truth and love? Is the tone one of discouragement or encouragement? The ethos of the church can be changed, and much of that comes from the pulpit, where the preacher, through the Holy Spirit, works to elevate the culture.

Knowledge of this world will guide the preacher in determining what passages and what series would best elevate the culture of the church. Maybe it's time to reexamine 1 Corinthians 13 or have a look at gentleness in Philippians 4 or anger in the Sermon on the Mount.

Knowledge of churchplace culture not only informs the selection of preaching passages but also guides the ethos of the preacher. What do you sound like when you preach? Are you sarcastic or negative? Are you enthusiastic and full of life? Are you dull or, to use one of Haddon's favorite words for his least favorite trait, insipid? How do your listeners perceive you? As a credible person of character?

When we talk about ethos, we're talking about an appeal to the character and credibility of the speaker. From the pulpit, you create a culture of kindness and love and forgiveness. You can elevate ethos from the pulpit—by your selection of words and intonation and tone. The ethos you project from the pulpit can serve to elevate church culture and language.

## Evaluate, Appreciate, and Elevate Because of Love

I've presented many nerve-racking lectures in front of Haddon Robinson, and he evaluated me after every single one. Sometimes he said, "That didn't work," but then he'd tell me why and help me make adjustments and improvements.

Other times he'd smile and say, "Now *that* worked!" and he'd offer an explanation. Although his evaluation could be painful, he did it out of love—a love for the students and a love for those learning to teach them.

An early riser, Haddon always taught morning classes. When I was teaching with Haddon, I had a preschooler who attended the G. F. Brown School in Newburyport, Massachusetts, and I had to hustle to drop off my son and get to school on time. If you've ever done the get-kids-ready, drop-off/pick-up routine, you know the stress I'm talking about. When I arrived at class, Haddon always made an effort to ask me about drop-off at the "Brown" school. He inquired about what Jack was learning. "It's raccoons this week," I said. "What about raccoons?" he asked. "They're nocturnal and they eat garbage," I replied. Then he'd tell me that when he was a boy schools didn't have names like "Brown." He went to PS (public school) number such and such.

The conversation was short. It wasn't a big deal, but he was showing an interest in my morning and in my son. It was a practical way to express love. And love was important to Haddon. On the very first day I began working with him, Haddon invited me to his office. He was working on a sermon series from 1 Corinthians 13, and he told me that if he were known and remembered for anything, he hoped it would be love. He hoped he'd be known as a loving person. I was a bit surprised. Wouldn't he want to be known and remembered for his preaching or his teaching or his textbook? And quite honestly, love wasn't the first thing that came to my mind when I thought of Haddon. Smart, certainly. Consummate preacher and teacher, absolutely. Intimidating, for sure. Quick wit, definitely. But love? It wasn't my first inclination—until I got to know him. The aforementioned qualities still come to mind when I think of him, but now, love comes first.

One Tuesday morning when I walked into class, Haddon looked tired. He told me it was my fault that he was awake all night. He knew my mother was sick, and he had been praying for her. Tears filled my eyes as I thanked him. Unbeknownst to him, my mother's health had taken a turn for the worse Monday evening and we almost lost her during the night. But by Tuesday morning, her situation had drastically improved.

Haddon was concerned about the things that concerned me. I call that love.

Evaluate the history, culture, and language of your parishioners. Then you'll be able to address areas that need elevating and appreciate what's important to them, and the more opportunities you'll have to love them.

# 8

## The Mission of Preaching in This World

VICTOR D. ANDERSON

### Introduction

Whether you listened to Haddon Robinson preach, sat under his homiletics tutelage in a classroom, read his books, or chatted with him around the table, you came away with a sense that this man had an unusually high view of preaching. For him, preaching was not a little thing, not a minor instrument in God's symphony. Robinson's grand view of preaching inspired others wherever his voice traveled.[1]

In honor of Robinson's grand view of preaching, this chapter seeks to inspire readers to be enthralled with a similar perspective. Whether one is responding to a fresh, new call to preach or seeking to keep the plow in the field to deliver yet another sermon, a preacher finds renewed energy by holding a lofty view of preaching. And how it is needed today! A scan of current

1. Haddon Robinson invested nineteen years at Dallas Theological Seminary as a professor of homiletics, and the impact of that investment reverberates today through the halls of our institution. Though the sound of his voice no longer fills the corridors, I have keen awareness that our Department of Pastoral Ministries has been shaped for good by Haddon's teaching over the decades. The faculty in my department readily acknowledge a debt to this man who helped us think about preaching that touches lives deeply. We are grateful to Haddon for the good foundation that he laid.

resources for preachers may well cause us to think of preaching not as grand but as pragmatic, therapeutic, or reformative.

Pragmatists view preaching simply as a tool for achieving some concrete goal, like bigger offerings or more nursery volunteers. A recent electronic advertisement in my inbox urged me to click on a link that gave tips for "How to Fill Up Your Church This Easter," as if preaching was primarily a method for stimulating church attendance. Elsewhere, therapeutic preaching pundits see preaching primarily as counsel for helping individuals succeed in life. Preaching in this arena helps listeners overcome addictions, produce a better marriage, and develop happy, healthy families. Note how many times the words "victory," "success," and "how to . . ." appear in sermon titles and bulletin promotions. For some, preaching is essentially a tool for providing a moral compass in the present and salvation from hell in the future. Additionally, with the increasing visibility of societal ills, preaching in other quarters may be perceived as that which reforms communities, societies, and cultures.

While such views of preaching focus on specific needs that the pulpit may address, none of them constitutes a grand view of preaching. Church-building, self-improvement, moral development, and cultural reformation are but peepholes rather than a consuming vision. A grand vision of preaching comes through nothing less than seeing preaching as participation in the mission of God for our world.

## Preaching as the Mission of God

This brief chapter begins to cast such a grand vision for preaching by examining preaching as the mission of God. We survey key features of the mission of God and consider how the mission of preaching both declares and enacts the mission of God. The second aspect of our discussion focuses on preaching as mission to our present world—a fast-changing biosphere with long-standing needs. Strangely enough, our mission to this world transpires primarily through ministry to an audience called out from that world.

### The Mission of Preaching as Servant of the Mission of God

The title of this chapter, "The Mission of Preaching in This World," begs the question about the mission of preaching at all. As mentioned above, we may be tempted to conceive of the preaching mission primarily in terms of its intention toward the world or toward the audience as individuals. The suggestion here, however, is that the mission of preaching be considered first in relation to the mission of God. The very mission of God forms the mission of preaching. Having understood preaching in terms of God's mission, we are better positioned to grasp the mission of preaching (as God's mission) to the world.

Articulating the mission of God for the world is akin to asking for the big idea of the whole Bible. Taking the whole Bible as a unit with a grand textual intention (superintended by one Author), we perceive the subject of the Bible to be what God is doing with this world—in other words, the mission of God for this world. The Bible develops this subject with the contention that the Master's mission is to demonstrate his rule upon the earth through his people.[2] This is what God's mission is all about—bringing his rule to fruition on the earth and doing so through the agency of people whom he has called and transformed to be like himself. The data to inform us of God's mission come not from a single text but from the sweep of God's story, from Genesis 1 to Revelation 22.

The opening chapter of Genesis reaches its climax with the creation of humankind as the image of God.[3] While theologians discuss at length the various ontological features of humankind being fashioned in God's image, such discussions often miss the reality that an image by its very nature must image, reflect, or represent. The essence of an image is the function of imaging. Genesis 1 stresses that humankind, unlike the rest of creation, is to engage in this representational function to the rest of creation under God and for God. Further, this display of God's image is to fill the earth. In every crevice of creation, there is to be the manifestation of God himself through humankind. Here is the initiation of the mission of God—to see his proper representation everywhere.

While the rest of the Bible reveals additional facets of this imaging challenge, the core features are on full display in Genesis 1. Undoubtedly, the most prominent feature is the demonstration of God's rule upon the earth. We see it in the first utterances from God to humankind, a commission to fill the earth and *subdue* it, *ruling* over the fish, birds, and other created elements (vv. 26–28). We see God's rule on display through his own creative actions in the opening narrative. While this creative activity certainly demonstrates divine genius and power, the narrative thrust announces God as the ruler over all that exists by virtue of his ownership of it. Into dark, chaotic unruliness

2. Christopher J. H. Wright, *The Mission of God: Unlocking the Bible's Grand Narrative* (Downers Grove, IL: IVP Academic, 2006).

3. The narrative design of Gen. 1 clearly points to verses 26–28 as its climax. The rhythmic style that reports the creation of everything else is broken by God's statement, "Let us make mankind in our image." Humankind is different from all the rest of creation by virtue of the creative process as well as the subsequent unique commission.

(v. 2), God speaks order, and creation obeys as compliant servant. Ruling is on display. Likewise, God is portrayed as the rightful owner of this world. It is his world; he is sovereign over it and has all the rights of ownership. And wonder of wonders, God delegates his sovereign rule to a creature made of dust who will serve as regent. Like a king of the ancient Near East who conquered a foreign nation and left behind a statue to commemorate his sovereignty, so God who conquered the chaos of the primordial state left humankind as his statue to declare his sovereignty.

Therefore, here is the initial revelation of the mission of God. While this image-bearing role recurs throughout the unfolding narrative of Scripture, four subsequent texts mark out the continuation of the mission throughout the ages.[4] First, reminiscent of the inaugural commissioning of humankind in Genesis 1, God commissioned Israel to a privileged role of demonstrating his rule upon the earth.[5] Having grown his nation from the descendants of Abraham and delivered them from Egyptian oppression, thereby demonstrating his sovereign rule on the earth, Yahweh commissioned his embryonic nation to be "a kingdom of priests and a holy nation" (Exod. 19:4–6). With these words, Israel was launched on God's mission to fill the earth with demonstration of God's rule. While these words may seem disconnected from the mission of God declared in Genesis 1, they actually portend a close association to the creation narrative. A kingdom expresses rule, and in Israel's case, the rule to be expressed is not Israel's but Yahweh's. Israel's kingdom was to demonstrate the very kingdom of God on earth. Further, this kingdom was to carry a priestly function: mediation between God and the nations to bring the nations of the world into submission to the King of Israel. So both elements of the mission of God originally seen in Genesis 1 are rearticulated in Exodus 19 for Israel. The rule of God, originally channeled through Adam and his descendants, would now be routed through the kingdom of Israel. Second, the reach of the mandate to "fill the earth" is redirected through Israel in the concept of a priestly function of this nation to all other nations.

---

4. Although Adam and Eve initiate humankind into a consistently rebellious challenge to God's mission by being image usurper rather than image bearer, the mission itself continues. This continuation is evident in Gen. 9, where Noah is recommissioned as a new Adam who is to fill the earth with image bearers who demonstrate God's rule. Further, when this earth-filling rule is most threatened by the tower builders on the plain of Shinar, God intervened to ensure scattering throughout the earth (Gen. 11:1–9) and then call Abram (Gen. 12) in initiation of the elevation of the people of Israel as image bearers.

5. If image bearing is relegated to ontological concerns, the reader misses the idea that Israel and the church are designated for image-bearing functions, even though they are not human beings. The image of God is made visible not simply by individuals but by these God-ordained institutions.

This earth-filling scope for Israel's mission appears first in the Abrahamic covenant and later in the establishment of the temple for Israel and foreigners to approach God and worship him.

Israel's refusal to function as God's kingdom of priests results in exile for the nation, destruction of the temple, loss of the law, and decimation of the reign of its kings.[6] The end of the Old Testament indicates that, despite reoccupation of the land and a rebuilt temple, the kingdom of God is not filling the earth. Malachi's cry to Israel is to shut the temple door, signaling that chaos not unlike that of Genesis 1:2 and 11:9 has returned to the earth. For the next four centuries, the rule of God fails to be evident on the earth.

Into the ruins of Israel's failed mission, God sent Jesus as the superior "image of the invisible God" who would have supremacy in all things (Col. 1:15–16). Both John the Baptist (Matt. 3:2) and Jesus himself (Matt. 4:17) introduced Jesus as the one ushering in the kingdom of God. Indeed, Jesus displayed God's kingdom rule by repeatedly turning chaos into order and advancing life in the face of death. He called his disciples to pray for the kingdom to fill the earth, and he cleansed the temple of those who worked against foreigners coming to worship God as king of the earth. Yet despite Jesus's consistent declaration and demonstration of God's rule, his brief tenure in Palestine would not fill the earth with the image of God. For instead of embracing the rule of God offered through the rightful king of the earth, Jews and gentiles together killed Jesus. The evil chaos of that day was symbolized by the sun's refusal to shine on the afternoon of the crucifixion and the stone sealing shut the tomb in darkness. Humankind's rebellion against the Son of God exemplified its rebellion against the mission of God.

The mission of God—to demonstrate his rule upon the earth through his people—seemed all but lost with the crucifixion of the Messiah. Yet beginning with the resurrection and ascension of Jesus, God orchestrated a series of interventions to elevate another vehicle for demonstrating his rule upon the earth. This new multiethnic vehicle—the church—replaced Israel as the privileged representative of God's image upon the earth (Matt. 21:43). The church, functioning as a refashioned kingdom of priests (1 Pet. 2:9), was commissioned to display the rule of God throughout the earth. Indeed, God has positioned the church as a spiritual temple to manifest the presence of God and mediate between God and the world (1 Pet. 2:4–5). Therefore, the mission

---

6. There is striking similarity between the rebellion of Adam and Eve (Gen. 3) and Israel's rejection of its mission to function as a kingdom of priests. In the garden of Eden, the couple chose to be like God rather than to represent God to the world. Likewise, in choosing idolatry (particularly fashioning its own gods) and in trying to be like other nations, Israel rebelled against the mission of representing Yahweh to the world.

of God, seemingly crushed with the rejection of Jesus, continues through the church, moving ever outward to fill the earth with a demonstration of the rule of God.

The church, though well equipped with Word and Spirit, will not complete this mission of filling the earth with the rule of God. A rule of darkness will eventually cover the earth. At a time of global economic prosperity and global religious unity, the final antichrist deceives the citizens of earth into believing that the rule of God has finally arrived. This faux light sets the scene for the climactic intervention of Christ himself. And in this climactic intervention, the evil one is destroyed and the curse removed. Ultimately, a new heaven and new earth will provide the arena for the rule of Christ to cover the earth through his people (Rev. 22:1–5). The throne of the Lamb shall occupy the central position of earth, as chaos and evil are banished (symbolized by the absence of sea and darkness, respectively) from his kingdom. The people occupying this kingdom are qualified as true image bearers of God, for they have become like the ultimate image bearer, Christ himself (1 John 3:2). All residents of this new kingdom have the identity of the King prominently on display, characterized by the apostle John as having his name written on their foreheads (Rev. 22:4). And at last he shall rule the earth through his people (Rev. 22:5).

In sum, the mission of God, initiated in Genesis 1, reiterated throughout Scripture, and climaxed in Revelation 22, is to demonstrate the rule of God everywhere on earth through his people, headed up by King Jesus himself. This mission of God is that which forms the mission of preaching. To say it another way, we ought to conceive of the mission of preaching as an important expression of the mission of God in our day. This is true in at least two ways: declaration and execution.

### The Mission of Preaching as Declaration of the Mission of God

The preceding paragraphs argued that from beginning to end, the big idea of the Bible centers on the mission of God. At some points, God's mission languishes in the rebellion of humankind; at others, it advances, particularly with the intervention of God. Every page of the Bible informs us of our responsibility as image bearers, celebrates the display of God's image, and/ or rebukes humans for their choices to replace God's image with their own. Since that is the central declaration of the whole text, preachers would do well to consider how exposition of every smaller text touches on this core idea. The mission of preaching is to declare this mission of God. Such conviction anchored the initial proclamations of John the Baptist and Jesus.

"Repent, for the kingdom of heaven has come near" (Matt. 3:2). So rang out the message of John the Baptist as he prepared the way for God's king to go public. With nearly identical words, the inaugural message of Jesus in Mark's Gospel echoes the words of John. "The kingdom of God has come near. Repent and believe the good news" (Mark 1:15). Both of these one-sentence sermons declare the reality of the kingdom and invite hearers to participate in it. With the advent of Jesus, the King came near, so the kingdom was at hand. This new display of the kingdom was, in Jesus's words, "good news." The news was not about crucifixion, resurrection, and atonement; rather, it was the recognition that the mission of God did not die with Israel's failure but would continue with this King sent from heaven.

These two texts from the opening chapters of Matthew and Mark certainly were not written to explain the mission of preaching per se. Yet their positions at the head of these Gospels and their utterances from the lips of the prophet and the King support the contention that the mission of preaching is intimately bound to the declaration of the mission of God to bring his rule to the earth through his King and ultimately through his people. Coming out of four hundred years of dark silence from the end of the Old Testament, these statements from John the Baptist and from Jesus announce renewed zeal for visible demonstration of God's kingdom. The King has come and the program of God has shifted into a higher gear, so to speak.

The argument here is that the prevalence of the mission of God from the Bible's beginning to its end, reinforced by the exemplary messages of John the Baptist and Jesus, provides preachers today with a grand view of preaching that centers on the mission of God in this world. As preachers unpack pericope after pericope each week for their congregations, they unveil small portions of this all-encompassing mission of God. Whether the message comes from an Old Testament text, from a section of the Gospels, or from a sliver of the Epistles, it declares in some way, "Repent, for the kingdom of God draws near." Of course, the content of today's expositions come from a wide range of Bible texts, most of which do not directly speak about the rule of God or his kingdom. Yet the mission of God is never far from the content of biblical sermons. The preacher's privilege is to declare repeatedly the rule of this God who presses order into chaos and who gives life in the face of death. Such aspects of the mission of God frequently present themselves in texts in which God defeats enemies of his people, whether those enemies are people, diseases, or spirits. The justice of God speaks not simply of a divine attribute; rather, it declares that God's rule is to be displayed on the earth and promotes full experience of life for those who otherwise have been deprived of it.

In a similar fashion, creation's longing for life the way it ought to be occurs repeatedly in Scripture, hearkening to the reality that God will one day complete his mission. Every text that addresses the problem of sin carries an implicit hope for a world to come that is free from the curse. Every text that speaks of salvation, whether in terms of justification, forgiveness, or union with Christ, speaks not only of present reality but of a future completion that should fill believers with hope. The mission of preaching is to stimulate faith and hope in this coming reality where the rule of God through his people covers the earth. In the words of Barry Jones, we set before people a captivating vision for completion of the mission of God. According to Jones, this vision is no less than the vision of God:

> This vision [of God] is unveiled in the biblical account of creation in the first two chapters of the Bible, Genesis 1–2, and strikingly depicted through those biblical texts that anticipate the creation's glorious renewal, most notably in the final two chapters of the Bible, Revelation 21–22. In this sense, we might say that the *visio Dei* is the vision that the *missio Dei* seeks to realize. God's action in history, most notably in the incarnation, has been for the purpose of realizing this vision.[7]

Finally, we think of the climactic manner in which Christ the King is proclaimed through preaching. Many texts directly address the person and work of Christ. Others urge us to be like him, whether by direct command in the New Testament or through a Christo-iconic linkage in the Old Testament.[8] Still others point to the future completion of our transformation to Christlikeness and our role of reigning with him. In all such references, sermon content establishes a connection, whether explicitly or implicitly, to the mission of God as we deal with the one who is the image of God par excellence. We point to Jesus's words and works as those that most closely display the words and works of God himself. We preach Jesus as the object of our aspiration, and we are preaching him as the image of God whom we must imitate. We speak of Jesus as King and Ruler, thereby proclaiming that the rule of God comes to earth in physical form through this man. In preaching Jesus, we preach the advancement of the mission of God to fill the earth with God's image through his people.

In sum, the foregoing discussion advocates that the mission of preaching is a declaration of the mission of God. The mission of God is not an occasional

---

7. Barry Jones, *Dwell: Life with God for the World* (Downers Grove, IL: InterVarsity, 2014), 32–33.

8. Abraham Kuruvilla, *Privilege the Text! A Theological Hermeneutic for Preaching* (Chicago: Moody, 2013).

topic or subtopic of our sermons; rather, it always forms the core content of our sermons, whether or not we realize it or refer directly to it.

### The Mission of Preaching as Execution of the Mission of God

While preaching seeks to *declare* the mission of God, it also *executes* the mission of God. In other words, the mission of preaching links closely to the mission of God not only because contents of the missions are entwined but also because of corresponding achievements. The mission of preaching is to advance the mission of God through its very action for or participation in God's mission. We see this participation in three different ways: creating individual image bearers, manifesting the presence of God, and displaying corporate image bearing.

First, preaching advances the mission of God by developing individual image bearers. In other words, preaching stimulates people to represent God more fully, as Christ himself represented his Father. This stimulation toward image bearing begins with regeneration through the initial call to repentance. While regeneration of people certainly occurs by the sovereign work of the Spirit of God, this work takes place through preaching of the Spirit-inspired Word. The initial call to repentance is the birthing of a life newly aligned with God and his mission, hearkening back to the creation event of Genesis 1. The Creator of life works through this spoken word to replicate origin of life. With each act of regeneration, individuals receive new life that truly frees that person to bear God's image as never before possible. Additionally, as people submit to the Word of God with each sermon, they are transformed slowly but certainly into Christlikeness (Rom. 8:29). Preaching in this vein is transformative, and the direction of that transformation is the direction articulated as the mission of God—creating Godlikeness, which we now know as Christlikeness. Kuruvilla says it well in his book *A Vision for Preaching*: "And that is God's ultimate intention, to conform his children to the image of Jesus Christ, his Son. All believers are headed in this direction in God's plan. Preaching facilitates this divine plan to conform believers to the image of the incarnate Word by the exposition of the written word, and so preaching is *conformational*."[9]

Preaching thus advances the mission of God by its creation of individual image bearers. At the same time, preaching is participation in the mission of God in that it manifests the presence of God. In this sense, preaching is sacramental; it provides an arena in which listeners may be sensitized to the presence of God. Preaching, we might say, provides an experience of heaven on earth.

9. Abraham Kuruvilla, *A Vision for Preaching: Understanding the Heart of Pastoral Ministry* (Grand Rapids: Baker Academic, 2015), 132 (emphasis original).

This is not to say that preaching utilizes some magical action or manipulation to cause the appearance of God. Actions of humans have no such leverage over God. Rather, God chooses to use preaching, much as he employs baptism and the Lord's Supper, to make known elements of his presence that otherwise often remain hidden. To the degree that it communicates the intention of God's Spirit, preaching converts mere words of man to divine Word—that is, the expression of the very presence and will of God. In this sense, preaching is epiphany. In the words of a teacher of Orthodox priests, that which is sacramental "not only 'posits' the idea of God as a rationally acceptable cause of its existence, but truly 'speaks' of Him and is in itself an essential means both of knowledge of God and [of] communion with Him, and to be so is its true nature and its ultimate destiny."[10] If we think of preaching in such terms, we see preaching as a powerful and mysterious mode through which God intervenes into earth's space and time. This is the true nature of preaching. Delivery of the sermon thus is not simply a communication act or persuasive speech; rather, it is a means by which the listener experiences real fellowship with God.[11] In terms of learning theory, such knowledge of God's presence is not and cannot be acquired simply by *comprehension* of ideas; rather, it comes by *apprehension* of the real presence of God through the proclamation.[12] As the people of God listen to the preached Word, they experience the real presence of Christ in a manner similar to what happens in the church's participation in the Lord's Supper.[13] In this way, preaching advances the mission of God, in a sense invoking the rule of God to be envisioned more readily upon the earth.

We have been describing how the mission of preaching is an active participation in the mission of God by creating image bearers and manifesting the presence of God. A third way that preaching advances the mission of God is by its action within the gathered people of God. Preaching is a

10. Alexander Schmemann, *For the Life of the World: Sacraments and Orthodox* (Yonkers, NY: St. Vladimir's Seminary Press, 2000), Kindle ed., locations 1718–19.

11. While the present argument is being made from a theological perspective, I have no doubt that certain cultures are more likely to realize that preaching is an experience of worship and fellowship with a God who is present in the event. For additional development of the cultural basis for this idea, see Victor D. Anderson, "Learning from African Preachers: Preaching as Worship Experience," *Journal of the Evangelical Homiletics Society* 10, no. 2 (September 2010): 83–104.

12. In D. A. Kolb's model of learning theory, comprehension and apprehension are at opposing poles of knowledge acquisition. Yet they do not operate exclusively of one another. In a preaching event, apprehension of God's presence works in conjunction with comprehension of God's truth to provide a sacramental effect for the listener. See Kolb, *Experiential Learning: Experience as the Source of Learning and Development* (Englewood Cliffs, NJ: Prentice-Hall, 1984).

13. For a helpful, concise defense of preaching as sacramental, see Kuruvilla, *A Vision for Preaching*, 58–66. This treatment also compares preaching and the Lord's Supper in a favorable manner with regard to their sacramental nature.

critical component of demonstrating the image of God through the meeting of the local assembly. We begin with the recollection that image bearing is not limited to individual human beings (as demonstrated in the first section of this chapter). In fact, imaging of God simply cannot be fully accomplished through individual expression. Rather, institutional gatherings of the people of God, first as the nation of Israel and then as the church, exercise privilege as unique expressions of God's rule upon the earth.

How does that work? The church, called out from a world of chaos and evil and gathered in submission to the preached Word of God, expresses the rule of God upon the earth. This display of God's order out of chaos is manifested by disordered lives corporately submitting to the order of declared Scripture. Here, in the proclamation of the Word, the Genesis 1 rule of God is reenacted as listeners experience creation and stimulation of their spiritual life. As a church affirms the proclaimed truth, it creates a visible expression of the maturing body of Christ—the image of God! Indeed, in Ephesians 4 the apostle Paul describes the creation of unity around the declaration of truth as a unique presentation of the person of Christ: "So Christ himself gave the apostles, the prophets, the evangelists, the pastors and teachers, to equip his people for works of service, so that the body of Christ may be built up until we all reach unity in the faith and in the knowledge of the Son of God and become mature, *attaining to the whole measure of the fullness of Christ*" (Eph. 4:11–13).

In this text, Paul connected the proclamation of truth to the maturing unity of the body of Christ. Set in the context of those called out from the world, the church-in-submission demonstrates the presence of Christ active on earth. The mission of God moves forward through preaching in the assembly.

In a similar fashion, weekly submission to the preached Word functions in the gathered church as liturgy. This liturgical function demonstrates the rule of God by increasing the desires of God's people for the full expression of the kingdom. As Jamie Smith points out, the physical act of experiencing the preached Word is formative for desires. The outward discipline effects an inward desire. As inherently desiring creatures, people habitually attending to sermons are thereby pulled less toward the world and more toward Christlikeness, not only in thinking and behavior but also in desire. In hearing sermons, submission to God's Word is practiced as a corporate act. There is a formative effect in people responding together, "We will do what God says." In this sense, engagement in the mission of preaching accomplishes the mission of God, creating longing for the rule of God through Christ and for the establishment of the good life. Smith aptly connects this idea to the manner in which preaching works to establish a narrative into which a believer's life is absorbed.[14] The story of the Bible, the story of God's mission to the world, is proclaimed through preaching in such a way that listeners renarrate their lives together.

> Over time, when worship confronts us with the canonical range of Scripture, coupled with its proclamation and elucidation in the sermon, we begin to absorb the story as a moral or ethical compass—not because it discloses to us abstract, ahistorical moral axioms, but because it narrates the *telos* of creation, the shape of the kingdom we're looking for, thus filling in the *telos* of our own action. We begin to absorb the plot of the story, begin to see ourselves as characters within it; the habits and practices of its heroes function as exemplars, providing guidance as we are trained in virtue, becoming a people with a disposition to "the good" as it's envisioned in the story. Because we are story-telling animals, imbibing the story of Scripture is the primary way that our desire gets aimed at the kingdom.[15]

In sum, preaching in the corporate setting participates in the mission of God by creating a present, visible demonstration of the rule of God, thus establishing a unity centered on the expression of Christlikeness. Further, preaching as a liturgical practice in the corporate setting advances the mission of God by stirring longings in people for the good life that is experienced only with Christ's kingdom filling the earth.

### Summary of Preaching as the Mission of God

Properly engaged, the mission of preaching is never far from the mission of God. The story of God's mission centers on the demonstration of the rule of God covering the earth through his image bearers. Likewise, preaching informs people of this mission, calls people to participate in it, and even advances the mission of God. This provides us with a grand view of preaching, one that sees preaching as integrated into the very mission of God, not only in the content of its declaration but also in the execution of that mission. Preaching creates image bearers, manifests the presence of God, and advances kingdom rule in the assembly.

### The Mission of Preaching as Mission to This World

Since the mission of God is directed fundamentally toward his world, we must consider how preaching also is mission to this world. On the one hand,

---

14. See James K. A. Smith, *Desiring the Kingdom: Worship, Worldview, and Cultural Formation*, Cultural Liturgies (Grand Rapids: Baker Academic, 2009), 196.

15. Smith, *Desiring the Kingdom*, 196.

such a thought seems grandiose. Most preachers do not reach a worldwide audience, nor do they think of their sermons in terms of the mass of diverse cultures. In actual practice, our preaching is to a small slice of the world. The congregation on Sunday morning is our world. Effective pastoral preaching generally targets real people with real needs in a real church setting. A preacher, choosing to focus on the world at large rather than on the world sitting on pews in front of him or her, likely will produce a sermon less effective for all who hear it. The world at large is everywhere around us but is nowhere in terms of where people actually live. No one lives in the world at large. The mission of preaching is not to preach to that nondescript world.

Perhaps the first way to conceive of preaching as mission to the world is to see it as mission *for* the world. In other words, while the preacher does not provide sermons *to* the world at large, the mission of preaching is *for* the world(s) with which an audience will interact. The mission of preaching is directed immediately to the people within earshot and indirectly for the benefit of the entire world as the object of and stage for the mission of God. With such a perspective, the preacher can be enthralled by a vision of immense proportion, a worldwide scope, while being properly focused on a vision of immediate practical engagement, the local church.

Preaching focuses on an audience called out from the world but living in the world. That wider world, awash in captivating media, distracts both preacher and audience. Ours is a world hyper-focused on the present. Importance is defined primarily by the volume of the speaker and the boldness of the font. For this reason, preaching as mission in this world must always address the competing identities pulling at parishioners. In the context of the local church, preachers speak to congregants as the called-out people of God. We constantly set before listeners the honor of this distinction. God's people are different by calling—made alive for the purpose of image bearing and destined to be participants in that great day when all is made as it ought to be. This is a counter-narrative to the world in which people live, and our sermons must immerse people in that narrative. Preachers historically have urged listeners not to be like the world. But such sermons try to play with only a single note. Such preaching fails to see the mission of God as a story that offers people a different identity, a real reason to get out of bed in the morning, and a rationale for not being like a world that has a different tragic destiny. Preaching in this world wrestles the attention of listeners from the bombardments of instant messaging and instills in them a focus on that which endures.

While sermons are bent toward people called out from the world, they also must prepare people to walk in the worlds where they must actually live. God's people must be sensitized repeatedly to the ways that their cultures promote disobedience, always making rebellion against God socially acceptable. These cultures encompass offices, factories, schools, and the countless channels of entertainment. The cultures of disobedience extend from ball field to bar and from Facebook to the water cooler. The story of God's mission to the world is a story of God intervening in places where society has sanctioned that which is despicable to God. Sermons cannot sweeten this bitter reality. The mission of preaching, when properly aligned with the mission of God, is to show the world in its true light. Preaching reorients people to a world that is in ongoing rebellion against the Creator, who possesses all the rights of ownership. Yet it simultaneously instills in them a sense of partnering with this Creator and his people, constantly casting before them a vision for a world set right by the presence and rule of the Lord Jesus Christ. The world is filled with people to be loved, not abandoned. Here is how the mission of preaching as the mission of God is mission to this world.

## Conclusion

Only the most challenging of tasks require a robust sense of mission. Preaching is such a task. Without a grand sense of mission, we likely will lose heart and give up our striving. This chapter has sought to inspire preachers to adopt a sense of mission for preaching that may sustain them in the midst of deepwater challenges. For the mission of preaching is akin to the mission of God. In its declaration and in its performance, preaching seeks to see the image of God filling the earth. It is a mission that causes us to grasp our God-designed purpose in history and anticipate its fulfillment in the future. And it is a mission that requires our focused attention on this present world as we represent God for the benefit of God's world.

# 9

## The World of History
## and the Task of Preaching

SCOTT WENIG

### Introduction

It is said that the great Reformation historian Heiko Oberman always told
his students, "You can't understand Luther and Calvin if you don't recognize
that they lived in a time when they could go to bed, die in the night, and end
up face to face with the Sovereign God. Without the advantages of modern
medicine they confronted temporal and spiritual realities most of us can't
even imagine." Contemporary preachers would be well advised to heed the
point of Oberman's admonition: we cannot understand how to preach the
Bible accurately and effectively if we don't know its history. Our sermons
might be relevant, astute, and even engaging, but if we ignore the history
behind the text, the full counsel of God contained in Scripture will almost
certainly be minimized.

   An anecdote from my own family might help to illuminate the underappreci-
ated value of historical knowledge. My dad served in the United States Army
Air Force in England and Germany from early 1943 through late 1945. As I
was growing up, he would occasionally speak of his wartime experiences, but
like most veterans of World War II, he mostly kept quiet about that part of his
life. My dad passed away long ago, but in 2003 a distant cousin sent me some

letters written by my dad to her mother (my dad's aunt) while he was overseas during the war. In those now treasured texts, I saw glimpses of a man whom I partially knew, but also discerned a younger man I knew little about. I came to know a soldier who, in the midst of hard times and a lonely place, was filled with gratitude for the cookies and cake his aunt sent him and who generously shared that sweet bounty with his comrades in arms. I also read the words of a young man who desperately wanted to return home but knew he had a duty to fulfill. When I grew up, I came to know my dad as a man, but I never knew that other part of him until I understood that piece of his personal history.

## What History Is and Why It Is So Important

So what exactly is history? And why do preachers of the Bible need to give it time and attention? Former archbishop of Canterbury Rowan Williams defined history as a story that allows us to better understand who we are and the world we live in.[1] Another way to understand history is to view it as a discipline that seeks to reconstruct the past.[2] But as one investigates the past, biblical or otherwise, it becomes increasingly clear that the past is like a foreign country. Historian David Lowenthal demonstrated this perfectly in his story of the midwestern American businessman who visited Plimoth Plantation, the Massachusetts museum of history specializing in the seventeenth-century settlement of New England. There Lowenthal witnessed this businessman—a booster of individualism and free enterprise—engaged in an encounter with an actor playing William Bradford, the governor of Plymouth colony. As Lowenthal notes:

> Like many Americans, this visitor grew up in the faith that the Pilgrim Fathers were true begetters of his own values. Now he was finding *this* prototype Father's views diametrically opposed to his own. Bradford was a Calvinist predestinarian, a believer in community to whom secular capitalist enterprise was blasphemous, selfish individualism anathema. Seething with indignation, the visitor could not just dismiss pious Bradford as a crank or a Communist. . . . For the first time in his life, this visitor confronted a world view fundamentally at odds with his own and had to engage with it as an idea.[3]

1. Rowan Williams, *Why Study the Past: The Quest for the Historical Church* (Grand Rapids: Eerdmans, 2005), 1.
2. John Fea, *Why Study History? Reflecting on the Importance of the Past* (Grand Rapids: Baker Academic, 2013), 3.
3. David Lowenthal, "Dilemmas and Delights of Learning History," in *Knowing, Teaching and Learning History: National and International Perspectives*, ed. Peter N. Stearns, Peter Seixas, and Sam Wineburg (New York: New York University Press, 2000), 74–75 (emphasis original).

When preachers come to Scripture, they're engaging a series of texts that were produced a long time ago in a world far, far away. Whether the text is from that portion of the Bible that we call "old" or "first" or from the "new," the text is quite literally from a foreign country. It was originally written in a different language to an audience that lived at a time and in a place that can feel alien to the contemporary preacher, let alone to the average reader. To bridge those various gaps, the preacher *must* attend to the history of the text that will be preached.

This task may be even more important now than in previous generations. Despite the vast sales of current popular and scholarly historical monographs such as Ron Chernow's masterful *Alexander Hamilton*, we live in an age known for its historical amnesia.[4] Major universities in the United States no longer require courses in Western civilization or American history. And evangelical seminaries, in their attempts to attract and maintain students, have whittled down the church history portions of their curriculums to a bare minimum. Yet the writers of the Bible took history seriously! This is clearly seen by the very deliberate and careful approach they took in constructing their accounts of the past. The historical books of the Bible in general, and the history behind all the other books in particular, were written with the assumption that knowing the past was vitally important to the life, identity, and spiritual health of God's people. As Old Testament scholar Patricia Dutcher-Walls says:

> Knowing about the past addressed and showed concern for the situation of the audience and its social institutions, roles, leaders, political decisions, events and peoples. Biblical historiography addressed its contemporaries through the fascinating stories being told, through the theological interests being communicated, and through the ways the accounts of the past were conveyed. It is clear that all these stories of the past, with their artistry and persuasiveness, with their insistent explanations, points of view, and values were . . . important, and the past of this people with their God was worth remembering.[5]

In their unique ways, all of the biblical authors were making a contribution to the long, continuous story of God's plan to redeem his fallen creation. The Bible records innumerable historical events on which the truth of our faith is based. To the Jews and the first Christians, history *always* mattered.

---

4. Ron Chernow, *Alexander Hamilton* (New York: Penguin, 2004). As of June 2016, more than one million copies of this book have been sold. See Joselyn McClurg, "Two Books about Hamilton Get Tonys Boost," *USA Today*, http://www.usatoday.com/story/life/books/2016/06/22/hamilton-lin-manuel-miranda-ron-chernow-usa-today-best-selling-books/86177750/.

5. Patricia Dutcher-Walls, *Reading the Historical Books: A Student's Guide to Engaging the Biblical Text* (Grand Rapids: Baker Academic, 2014), 172.

Innumerable examples could be cited to demonstrate this truth, but for our purposes here, two will suffice.

First, Matthew begins his Gospel—his history of the ministry, death, and resurrection of Christ—with a genealogy (Matt. 1:1–17). Modern readers of this text sometimes scratch their heads in curiosity about this introduction. Why bother to give readers a list of name after name after name from the Old Testament that finally ends with a statement about Jesus's parents, Joseph and Mary? Matthew's larger goal in his Gospel was to demonstrate to his Hebrew readers that Jesus was the promised and long-awaited Messiah. As every Jew had been taught since childhood, the Messiah was to come from the tribe of Judah and be the son of David, Israel's greatest king. Matthew's genealogy lays out Jesus's lineage to demonstrate the viability of his messianic claim by rooting it in his *historical and familial descent* from the patriarchs and David.

Second, let us take a moment to review how Luke introduces his Gospel to its original recipient, Theophilus: "Many have undertaken to draw up an account of the things that have been fulfilled among us, just as they were handed down to us by those who from the first were eyewitnesses and servants of the word. With this in mind, since I myself have carefully investigated everything from the beginning, I too decided to write an orderly account for you, most excellent Theophilus, so that you may know the certainty of the things you have been taught" (Luke 1:1–4).

Innumerable commentators and biblical apologists have pointed out that Luke followed a carefully guided historiographic procedure in the composition of his Gospel. He seems to have gathered a variety of sources and then proceeded with a detailed investigation of the claims made by these sources, be they documentary or personal accounts that were given to him orally. Having established the historical viability of Jesus's life, death, and resurrection, he then composed his Gospel to undergird the faith of his readers. As one scholar cleverly noted, "Here we have Luke's self-assessment of his literary work: he has done his homework and he has done it well."[6]

The past, biblical or secular, is certainly something of a foreign country to many of our congregants, and it may be as well to those of us who preach. That means we must function as travel guides to the distant countries of the Bible's origins to understand what the Holy Spirit was communicating to God's people in the various venues and eras in which Scripture was composed. If we are going to effectively leverage the pulpit to evangelize, teach, and disciple

---

6. Joel B. Green, *How to Read the Gospels and Acts* (Downers Grove, IL: InterVarsity, 1987), 75.

a generation or two of people who have little or no knowledge of Scripture, we *must* give serious and studied attention to its history.

## To Understand a Text, We Must Know the History Behind the Text

All of us who preach the Scriptures deeply desire that our sermons will inspire our listeners to apply the Bible so that, by God's grace, their lives will be transformed into the likeness of Christ. No less a preacher than the apostle Paul once claimed, "He is the one we proclaim, admonishing and teaching everyone with all wisdom, so that we may present everyone fully mature in Christ. To this end I strenuously contend with all the energy Christ so power-fully works in me" (Col. 1:28–29). As Paul clearly implies by his use of the phrase "I strenuously contend with all the energy Christ so powerfully works in me," spiritual transformation does not happen easily, instantaneously, or magically; it happens only when God's Spirit is at work in the preacher, the preaching, and the hearers over a long period of time. I do not think we can demand of God that he automatically bless our preaching every time we ascend the pulpit or communicate his Word from behind the music stand. What we can do is ensure that we give proper attention to the text and the history behind it as we prepare.

As I tried to demonstrate earlier, the various worlds of the Bible—whether the ancient Canaan and Egypt of the patriarchs, the Babylonian and Persian empires of the sixth century BC, or the cities of the Eastern Mediterranean that Paul inhabited in the first century AD—were vastly different from our own. To understand the Bible correctly, "We must 'mind the gap' as the trains in London say—the gap between ourselves and the ancient world of the biblical author and their audiences."[7] This requires that when we approach Scripture, we recognize those gaps and get a clear sense of what the biblical text meant in its own time and place. Paying close attention to the historical distance between ourselves and the past prevents us from adopting naive interpreta-tions and strained applications, such as equating New Testament slavery with modern workers at Apple, or ancient temples with contemporary churches.[8]

To understand what a text meant when it was written, we must reconstruct its historical context to the best of our ability, utilizing the archaeological, linguistic, and literary evidence at our disposal.[9] This pushes back against

7. Michael Bird, "Neglecting the Cultural Divide," *Bible Study Magazine*, November 2016, 32.
8. Bird, "Neglecting the Cultural Divide," 32.
9. Robert B. Chisholm Jr., *From Exegesis to Exposition: A Practical Guide to Using Biblical Hebrew* (Grand Rapids: Baker, 1999), 151.

our own innate "reader-oriented analysis" that seeks to make the biblical world similar to our world of the twenty-first century and unintentionally undermines the authority and veracity of the text. Take, for example, the fascinating story in Genesis 23 of Abraham's negotiation with the Hittites for a burial plot for his deceased spouse, Sarah. On the surface, this narrative raises all kinds of questions. Why does the Bible contain a text that doesn't mention God? Why do we need to know about an ancient Hebrew sheik's interaction with a strange people group over a plot of land? Why would we bother to teach from this text to all those overly busy and stressed-out Americans who inhabit our churches on the weekends? I'd like to suggest that this story is tremendously *relevant* to us, but only as we understand the history behind the text.

On a first reading it appears that the Hittites are humbly denying Abraham's request because he lives as a great lord among them. On closer examination of the historical setting in the ancient Near East, however, we see that is not the case at all. This, in fact, is a classic example of Middle Eastern bargaining; going back and forth until a price is settled on, and, as this text shows, the Hittites were experts at it. After some hard negotiating, Abraham pays them far more than the burial plot is worth, but we cannot get to that fact without knowing the history behind the text. Moreover, we cannot understand why Abraham would go to such great lengths and make such an enormous financial investment for a mere burial plot unless we remember the history of his life—the two great promises—one of the son, which was fulfilled in Isaac, and the second of the land, which was not fulfilled in his lifetime. The author wants us to know that Abraham paid a huge price for this tiny piece of land as an expression of faith that the Lord would, in his time and way, give it all to his people through the seed of Isaac. Functionally, Abraham was making a costly investment in the promised future of God's people, and that has profound consequences for Christian living—and giving—in the consumerist era of twenty-first-century America. But, once again, we cannot arrive at that homiletical point unless we first know the history of the place, the people, and the person recorded in the text.

A second example, the story of Zacchaeus in Luke 19, is more familiar but also reveals the necessity of understanding the historical setting of the text. Luke tells us that Jesus was passing through the city of Jericho on his way to Jerusalem when he encountered that "wee little man." Being short, Zacchaeus climbed a tree to see Jesus, who stopped and invited himself over for lunch. And at that lunch, Zacchaeus was converted into a follower of Christ. As every preacher knows, this is an amazing story of spiritual transformation, because Zacchaeus was not just anyone; he was a tax collector and thus a "bad guy" in the eyes of his society. But this is where the history behind the text helps us to understand the text in a far richer manner and get beyond the Sunday school tale of a small man who became a big Christian.

In the ancient empire of Rome, the government auctioned off bids to collect taxes in its provinces, with the job going to the highest bidder. And it is important to remember that Rome operated by a flat-tax policy; the individual who got the bid *had* to collect all the taxes or he got flattened! But once the tax collector fulfilled his imperial obligation, he could keep everything else he gathered from the people of the province. For the Jews living under Roman occupation, tax collectors were not just sinners, bad neighbors, or "bad guys"; they were the "worst of the worst" because they economically exploited their own people for vast personal gain. They sold out their ethnic brothers and sisters to the gentile oppressors in order to fill their own pockets. This meant that in Jewish society, tax collectors not only were hated but were deprived of their political and civil rights. They were not allowed to give testimony in court or serve as judges, and pious Jews would not come near them if at all possible.[10] Moreover, Zacchaeus was exceptionally competent in this despicable craft; we are told that he was the chief tax collector (Luke 19:2), meaning that he had others working for him. No wonder those who followed Jesus down that street in Jericho *grumbled* when he went to lunch with the little scoundrel! Zacchaeus was the ancient equivalent of a contemporary drug lord who made millions of dollars selling heroin and cocaine to teenagers. Neither Christ's intentionality in befriending him nor his shocking conversion can really hit home homiletically until we communicate the historical reality behind this amazing episode of unadulterated grace toward someone most of us would certainly despise.

## Language and Culture Are Historically Significant Parts of the Text

Evangelicals have traditionally argued that, as God's Word, the Bible has eternal relevance. By this we mean that it speaks to all people in every time, place, and culture of human history. But God deliberately chose to inspire its human authors, who lived at specific times and in various locations, to write exactly what God wanted to communicate. This concept is known as the "historical particularity" of Scripture; each book, poem, proverb, letter, prophecy, or parable is conditioned by the ancient language, context, and culture, as well as the personality of the human author, in which it was

10. Joachim Jeremias, *Jerusalem in the Time of Jesus* (Philadelphia: Fortress, 1989), 303–6.

composed. Thus Scripture is not only a divinely inspired document but also, in its very essence, a *historical* manuscript.[11]

As the Word of God, the Bible demands that we approach it with sacred reverence. And as a historical document, it demands that we treat it on its own terms with genuine respect. God's Word does speak to us in the twenty-first century, but it spoke first to its original audience through the inspired author. The original hearers or readers of a text, book, or prophecy were able to understand it because it was composed in their own language and cultural context. This fact has, at the very least, two major implications for those of us who take the Bible as our rule for faith and life and who preach and teach from it on a consistent basis.

First, we need to draw any and every insight we can glean from a biblical passage, text, or story by studying the original language in which it was composed. Language is fundamental to the literary analysis of Scripture because it not only shapes an author's thought but quite often reveals an author's intent more precisely than what we might gain from an English translation. For example, in the infamous story of David's moral descent recorded in 2 Samuel 11, the narrator uses the Hebrew verb *šālaḥ* (send) seven times with David as the subject. In his role as king, David sends Joab to battle; sends for Bathsheba to seduce her; sends for her husband, Uriah, to cover up the adultery; and when that fails, treacherously sends Uriah back to Joab, where he's put on the front lines and killed. By repeating this verb, the author communicates that David appears to be an all-powerful royal entity doing whatever he wants, even to the point of committing adultery, murder, and deception. But God does not sit idly by. He invokes judgment on David by sending the prophet Nathan (2 Sam. 12:1–14) to denounce David's actions and declare that he and his family will now pay a horrible price for his abuse of royal power. David now becomes powerless in the hands of the sovereign God as the judgment is played out. First, the child born to Bathsheba as a result of the adultery is stricken and dies (2 Sam. 12:15–18). Years later, David unwittingly sends his daughter Tamar to be raped by her brother (2 Sam. 13:7), and then he sends his son Amnon to an early death at the hands of another of his sons, Absalom (2 Sam. 13:27). It is possible to pick up this crucial nuance in an English translation, but in the Hebrew the repletion of *šālaḥ* shouts to the reader, highlighting the author's true intent.[12] As preachers we may not be as conversant in the original languages as we would like, but in the twenty-first

11. The essence of this paragraph is drawn from Gordon Fee and Douglas Stuart, *How to Read the Bible for All Its Worth*, 3rd ed. (Grand Rapids: Zondervan, 2003), 21–23.

12. Chisholm, *From Exegesis to Exposition*, 50; for a fuller analysis of this narrative and how it might be preached, see Scott A. Wenig, "A Different Exegetical and Homiletical Approach

century there are innumerable resources written and developed by brilliant biblical scholars that we can draw upon in our exegetical work. Given the abundance of these linguistic experts, many of whom are literally at our fingertips via Bible software, we would be wise to use them as much as we can.

A second implication of the historical particularity of the Bible for those of us who preach is its cultural relativity. Given that Scripture was composed in a wide variety of places over the span of at least 1,500 years, this should come as no surprise. The cultural context of Ruth and Boaz in the pre-monarchial era of Canaan was significantly different from that which Daniel and Ezekiel encountered in the Babylonian Empire of the sixth century BC. And the Hellenistic metropolis of Ephesus where Paul ministered in AD 60 was almost certainly more diverse in its cultural values and mores than either of the prior two. As Gordon Fee and Douglas Stuart have noted, the fact of cultural relativity in the historical documents of the Bible is a greater challenge to preachers—and homiletics professors like me—than we sometimes care to admit.[13] Take, for example, Paul's Epistle to the Galatians. While all the New Testament epistles were occasional documents from the first century, this one seems especially so.[14] Paul was furious that some false teachers had infiltrated the Asian churches that he and Barnabas had planted at great personal sacrifice. The false teachers were communicating that new converts to Christianity first had to become Jews via the rite of circumcision before they could be legitimate followers of Jesus. The Letter to the Galatians is seething in its dismissal of both this false soteriology and its perpetrators, even to the point of Paul's desire that they emasculate themselves (Gal. 5:12)! So how does that preach in the contemporary North American context with its emphasis on religious freedom, tolerance, and individual rights? While Paul's focus on the one true gospel is nonnegotiable, the Judaizers' emphasis on circumcision is a culturally relative issue that feels light-years from our own era and spiritual experiences. The book of Galatians can and should be taught in our current venues, but it demands that preachers recognize the historical and cultural relativity of its driving issue.

Perhaps less controversial but still of great importance is the issue of church government. Both Peter and Paul taught that the churches of the eastern Roman world were to be led by elders and deacons (1 Tim. 3; 5; Titus 1; 1 Pet. 5) and that

---

to a Prominent Biblical Narrative: Interpreting and Preaching 2 Samuel 11–12," *Journal of the Evangelical Homiletics Society* 10, no. 2 (September 2010): 7–26.

13. Fee and Stuart, *How to Read the Bible for All Its Worth*, 80.

14. Fee and Stuart, *How to Read the Bible for All Its Worth*, 58. This means that the letters were "occasioned" or called forth by some special circumstance on either the readers' side or the author's.

appears to be the polity that was adopted during the apostolic era. However, this is where biblical history and cultural relativity become enormously important for understanding both the Bible and its relevance to the contemporary era. By the end of the first century, almost all of the churches in the entire Roman Empire as well as those in the greater area of Syria and Parthia to the east had adopted an episcopal structure, with a bishop presiding over various congregations in a specific geographical region. One could deduce that they did so because they became ecclesiastically corrupt and departed from true apostolic practice. But it seems far more likely that they adopted the new structure because it was functionally more efficient given the *cultures* they inhabited. The people who lived in and around the Mediterranean and ancient Near East in the first few centuries of the Christian era were used to hierarchical structures of government. And given the fact that those churches continued to spread the gospel, rapidly reproduced themselves, and over the course of the next four centuries effectively infiltrated wide swaths of the world all the way from Spain to India, it appears that episcopal polity was generally functional.[15] This historical reality and its attendant cultural relativity make dictating any particular church polity from the New Testament as "the biblical model" problematic. A more useful—and accurate—approach might be to understand those Spirit-inspired epistles as teaching the necessity of godly leadership that can be structured in any culturally useful way so long as it promotes evangelism, congregational health, and the advance of God's kingdom (Acts 1:3–8).

## The Bible's Emphasis on the Value of Humanity and the Wonder of Redemption

Over the centuries various people have noted many disturbing elements within the Scriptures, such as the seemingly patriarchal oppression of women, the debauched polygamy of Hebrew kings like David and Solomon, and the apparent acceptance of slavery. Do all of these historical eccentricities contained in the Bible undermine its veracity and applicability to intelligent and enlightened people of the late modern world? I do not have the room within the confines of this chapter to make an apologetic for Scripture as the inspired and inerrant Word of God. People far more capable than I have already done that in a brilliant, winsome, and compelling fashion.[16] My goal

15. See Robert Louis Wilken, *The First Thousand Years: A Global History of Christianity* (New Haven: Yale University Press, 2012), 17–36.
16. For two examples among many, see Craig Blomberg, *Can We Still Believe the Bible? An Evangelical Engagement with Contemporary Questions* (Grand Rapids: Brazos, 2014); and

in this section is to focus on the fact that the history behind the Bible reveals its spectacular emphasis on the value of people and the wonder of God's gracious redemption.

For example, many people are bothered by the apparent lack of value ascribed to women in Scripture. Given the relative egalitarianism of contemporary American society, where women run Fortune 500 corporations, sit on the Supreme Court, and run for president, that concern is understandable. But if we get beyond the values and expectations of our culture to the reality of life for women in the ancient world, we may discover a different perspective. In the Greco-Roman world, there was a huge shortage of women: about 100 women for every 140 men. This discrepancy was the result of the pagan practice of infanticide, especially of baby girls. A first-century letter from a husband to his pregnant wife illustrates his concern for a hoped-for son versus a blatant disregard for a girl if one were to be delivered. "I ask and beg of you to take good care of our baby son. . . . If you are delivered of a child [before I come home] if it is a boy, keep it. If a girl, discard it."[17] As this disturbing example illustrates, women and especially baby girls in the ancient world were often discarded, abused, neglected, and killed. The early church took a visible stand in opposition to such practices by regularly rescuing female babies from this hideous historical practice.[18] It did so because of the example of Jesus *and* because of the teaching of the Bible that Jesus read: the Old Testament.

From the perspective of Scripture, women always had inherent value, since they were made in the image of God (Gen. 1:27). And because they reflected the *imago Dei*, women were, like men, agents of creative thought and vibrant action throughout Scripture. They were given a voice, made choices of all kinds, and impacted the flow of life and history. We see this in numerous historical vignettes: in the pain of marital rejection Leah turns her attention away from Jacob to God; in social desperation Tamar tricks Judah into a shocking pregnancy; in courageous faith Rahab hides the Hebrew spies; and in an act of sensual boldness Ruth nuzzles up to the feet of Boaz. Moreover, in the New Testament Luke tells about a number of women who, in contrast to their expected cultural behavior, traveled with and supported Jesus and his disciples out of their own private means (Luke 8:1–3)!

Scripture's teaching on marriage reinforces the revolutionary value that its authors ascribe to women. In the ancient world in general and the Greco-Roman

---

Matthew Richard Schlimm, *This Strange and Sacred Scripture: Wrestling with the Old Testament and Its Oddities* (Grand Rapids: Baker Academic, 2015).

17. Rodney Stark, *The Rise of Christianity: How the Obscure, Marginal Jesus Movement Became the Dominant Religious Force* (New York: HarperOne, 1996), 97–98.

18. Rodney Stark, *The Triumph of Christianity* (New York: HarperOne, 2011), 126–27.

world in particular, laws and cultural norms were designed to protect the sexual adventures of married men. A first-century writer now known as Pseudo-Demosthenes noted, "We have mistresses for our enjoyment, concubines to serve our needs and wives to bear legitimate children."[19] This opinion represents the norm of how women were viewed, used, and abused in the ancient world.[20]

In contrast, the Bible placed sexual practice and marriage in an entirely different framework from that of ancient cultural norms. Marriage was highly honored in both the Old and New Testaments, and adultery and sexual immorality severely censured (Song of Songs; Heb. 13:4). Reflecting God's original intent for marriage, Jesus taught on more than one occasion that "God 'made them male and female.' 'For this reason a man will leave his father and mother and be united to his wife, and the two will become one flesh.' So they are no longer two, but one flesh. Therefore what God has joined together, let no one separate" (Mark 10:6–9).

Building on this foundation, the apostles preached that husbands should love their wives as themselves, treat them with respect and dignity, and be emotionally and sexually faithful (Eph. 5:26–29; 1 Pet. 3:7; 1 Tim. 3:2). From cover to cover, Scripture unequivocally teaches the value of women and underlines the utter necessity of sexual fidelity within the confines of marriage.

So what are we to do with all those historical examples in the Bible of polygamy and the Bible's apparent affirmation of slavery? How do those passages preach? We need to confront them head-on, because they reveal the redemptive purposes of God and his incomprehensible love for his fallen, broken creatures. God appears to be more than willing to accommodate the sinful practices of human cultures in order to redeem and transform them *over time*. This redemptive effort reflects the divine grace that God consistently extends to all of humanity, most notably in the incarnation (John 1:1, 14). Thus, one of the first things we can teach about a practice such as polygamy is that it reflects the sinful nature of people who made it an accepted cultural practice of the ancient world. But we also need to point out that polygamy never worked! One need only look at the lives of Jacob, David, or Solomon as evidence of polygamy's disastrous moral and relational impact on entire families. And after the disappearance of Israel's monarchy following the Assyrian obliteration of the ten northern tribes and the Babylonian captivity

19. Quoted in Nancy Sorkin Rabinowitz and Lisa Auanger, eds., *Among Women: From the Homosocial to the Homoerotic in the Ancient World* (Austin: University of Texas Press, 2002), 293, cited by John Ortberg, *Who Is This Man? The Unpredictable Impact of the Inescapable Jesus* (Grand Rapids: Zondervan, 2012), 137.

20. See Ortberg, *Who Is This Man?*, 137–39, for a more detailed account.

of the remaining tribes of Judah and Benjamin, the practice of polygamy disappeared and is sanctioned nowhere in the New Testament.

Likewise, when it comes to an evaluation of slavery in the Bible, historical knowledge is indispensable. Our contemporary perception of slavery resides mostly in the fact of Africans being captured by English or Portuguese slave traders and then shipped to America, where the practice was institutionalized by the early eighteenth century.[21] Brutally oppressive and disgusting in all its various expressions, African American slavery in the antebellum South eventually facilitated the US Civil War. Slavery was legally eradicated with Lincoln's Emancipation Proclamation of 1863 and then functionally ended with the military defeat of the Confederacy in 1865, yet we continue to see the aftermath of its negative effects on our society in the early decades of the twenty-first century.[22]

In the ancient world, however, slavery was of a different nature. While ubiquitous, oppressive, and reflective of humanity's depravity, it was neither racial in origin nor necessarily for a lifetime. Slaves served in all kinds of capacities, including as teachers and mentors, and they could, in some circumstances, work or buy their way to freedom. Moreover, slavery was so much a part of the economic and social fabric of ancient societies that the inhabitants of those cultures, including the biblical authors, accepted it as a given (e.g., Eph. 6:5–9). Yet as one delves into the broader lessons in Scripture, it becomes increasingly apparent that there is a redemptive emphasis on slavery's ultimate eradication.[23] To cite one example, Paul makes the outrageous request that his friend Philemon accept back the latter's runaway slave, Onesimus, without any punishment and as a new brother in Christ (Philem. 1:8–21). This redemptive trajectory took centuries to be fully implemented, but over time the church lived it out in various social and cultural contexts. In fact, by the later medieval era, the ethos of freedom taught in the New Testament led to the wholesale eradication of slavery in western Europe.[24]

## Effective Preaching Requires That We Value History

Over the past decade or so, some outstanding scholars, popular historians, and sociologists have served the faith well by highlighting the darkness and depravity

21. See Hugh Thomas, *The Slave Trade: The Story of the Atlantic Slave Trade: 1440–1870* (New York: Simon & Schuster, 1997).

22. For a more detailed analysis of the history behind this, see James McPherson, *The War That Forged a Nation: Why the Civil War Still Matters* (Oxford: Oxford University Press, 2015), 173–91.

23. See William J. Webb, *Slaves, Women and Homosexuals: Exploring the Hermeneutics of Cultural Analysis* (Downers Grove, IL: InterVarsity, 2001).

24. Rodney Stark, *The Victory of Reason: How Christianity Led to Freedom, Capitalism, and Western Success* (New York: Random House, 2005), 3–32.

of the ancient world. While their stated goals have been to explicate the nature and practices of ancient civilizations, they have, in point of fact, revealed the tremendous progress of God's redemptive work, first through his chosen people, the Jews, and then through the promised Messiah, Jesus, and his church.[25] For example, in his magisterial work *A History of the Jews*, British historian Paul Johnson begins by explicating the corrupt depravity of the massive river civilizations of ancient Mesopotamia and Egypt with their utter reliance on human bondage and insane idolatry. It was in this environment that the Hebrews first heard from God through his revelation to the patriarchs, Moses, and the other prophets. And despite the innumerable moral and spiritual failures of God's chosen people, Johnson persuasively shows that the moral law of the Hebrew Scriptures began to transform not only God's own people but also various elements of the social, cultural, and political context of the ancient Near East.[26]

From a different angle and at a more popular level, Thomas Cahill likewise shows the enormous impact of God's people in his provocative work *The Gifts of the Jews*.[27] He focuses primarily on the ways that the Jews changed how humanity sees time, history, and themselves. The great civilizations of the ancient world—Egyptian, Mesopotamian, Greek, Roman—all possessed a cyclical view of history with an emphasis on fate. This created a certain degree of intellectual and emotional fragility that left humanity reeling from the belief that nothing fundamental about life could ever really change.[28] But the Jews challenged this belief and more, because their Scriptures told them that God had called them to be a transformative force in the world and that history was teleological. Moreover, inspired by their prophets and leaders, the Jews developed the revolutionary idea of personal destiny. As Cahill persuasively argues, "the very idea of *vocation*, of a personal destiny, is a Jewish idea."[29]

When Rodney Stark published his now iconic *The Rise of Christianity* in 1996, he was attempting to explain why the numerically tiny Jesus movement eventually took over the vast Roman Empire. As Stark's research shows, the world of ancient Rome was filthy, disease-ridden, idolatrous, misogynistic, and brutally violent.[30] This was the context in which the Savior was born, and his message of redemptive grace was preached first by the apostles and then by countless other men and women throughout every nook and cranny of the

25. Among others, C. S. Lewis brilliantly made this point in *Mere Christianity* (New York: Simon & Schuster, 1952), 54–55.

26. Paul Johnson, *A History of the Jews* (New York: Harper & Row, 1987), 3–124.

27. Thomas Cahill, *The Gifts of the Jews: How a Tribe of Desert Nomads Changed the Way Everyone Thinks and Feels* (New York: Doubleday, 1998).

28. Cahill, *Gifts of the Jews*, 5.

29. Cahill, *Gifts of the Jews*, 3 (emphasis original).

30. Stark, *Rise of Christianity*, 147–62.

empire. And through a series of chapters that reveal the utterly countercultural approach to life of the early church, Stark proved that Christianity, when lived out according to the guidelines expressed in Scripture, can actually transform an entire civilization.[31] When viewed from the perspective of its original historical context, the radical nature of Spirit-filled Christianity as portrayed in the New Testament takes on an entirely new meaning.

Tom Holland is a popular historian whose books on the decline of the Roman Republic and the origins of the Roman Empire unintentionally but brilliantly supplement Stark's work.[32] Whereas Stark focused his scholarly attention on the church, Holland dials in on the nature of Roman society and politics from the second century BC through the middle of the first century AD. Holland shows repeatedly that Roman culture glorified self-promotion, military conquest, authoritarian patriarchy, and sexual immorality of all kinds. Moreover, it was a culture in which violence was generally more accepted than vilified and power was the ultimate aphrodisiac. When the life and teaching of Jesus as well as the apostolic witness and the ethos of the New Testament are framed against this morally degenerate background, the sheer brilliance of the Christian faith shines anew.

## Conclusion

The historical realities vividly portrayed by these scholars and writers should make us want to preach the Bible in all its fullness every single week! Their work substantiates the enormous and often understated impact of God's Word not only on his people but also on the communities, cities, and cultures they inhabit. As we preach with an understanding of history and the historical worlds in which the Bible was formed, our exposition of the Scriptures will take on a greater depth of knowledge, insight, and power. It is said that when the Catholic biblical scholar Ronald Knox was a small boy, he suffered from insomnia. Asked what he did when he couldn't sleep, he replied, "I lie awake and think about the past."[33] Perhaps we as preachers should follow in his footsteps and think more about the past both in the middle of the night and on into the day! At the very least, we should all move toward a healthy study of history as a solid foundation for preaching the glorious Word of God.

31. Stark, *Rise of Christianity*, 209–15.
32. Tom Holland, *Rubicon: The Last Years of the Roman Republic* (New York: Random House, 2003); Holland, *Dynasty: The Rise and Fall of the House of Caesar* (New York: Random House, 2015).
33. Williams, *Why Study the Past?*, 4.

# 10

## Preaching to a Culture Dominated by Images

DONALD R. SUNUKJIAN

### Introduction

Sermons can seem boring when compared with movies. Attention seldom drifts during a video or a television program but often does during a sermon. When listeners are saturated all day long with visual images and pictures—magazine ads, billboards, computer pop-ups—how can a sermon of words connect and be effective?[1]

The popularity of radio programs and audiobooks points us toward an answer. An older generation can remember hunching spellbound by a radio as the Lone Ranger and Tonto, or Roy Rogers, or Gene Autry, or the Green Hornet confronted evil and brought justice. A contemporary generation has learned that audiobooks can make a long car ride bearable. Since these media also use only words, what makes them so gripping and effective?

---

1. While some visual or physical objects—e.g., PowerPoint, props, artistic creations developed on stage—might enhance the effectiveness of a message, our concern here is with only the verbal aspect of the preacher's message and how the preacher's words alone can impact a listener who is saturated with pictures all day long.

The answer, of course, is that their words paint pictures. Their words create visual images that the listeners *see* in their mind's eye.[2] A sermon can also do that. A sermon can generate visual images to keep the listeners attentive to God's truth.

Let me suggest, and illustrate, three ways we can paint the pictures that will keep people listening.

### Expand on the Biblical Author's Original Images

In Psalm 15, the author's original image is a tent. David asks, "LORD, who may dwell in your sacred tent? Who may live on your holy mountain?" (v. 1). The sermon can help the contemporary listener visualize the "tent" of ancient Israel:

> David is imagining that God, like a desert sheik, has a very large tent in which he lives—poles extended, flaps draped, people moving around, pots cooking, camels under the trees, Persian rugs, brass goblets, and large couches. The tabernacle is God's home, God's tent.
>
> And when David says, "Lord, who may *dwell* in your sacred tent?" he's saying, "Lord, who would you welcome for a visit in your tent?" The word *dwell* means to come by for a visit, to drop by for a few hours. "God, who would you be glad to have over for a few hours? Who would you love to spend some time with?" To *dwell* is temporary, meaning to spend a bit of time with.
>
> But then, in the second line, David makes it a longer visit—someone who stays not just for a few hours but for several days. When he asks, "Who may *live* on your holy mountain?" the word *live* means stay overnight, hang around for a few weeks, become part of the family, sort of live there permanently.
>
> That's our question: Lord, who do you welcome to spend some time with you? Who are you glad to see? Who would you be so delighted to have around, not just to visit, but to stay longer, maybe spend the night, or even stay for a few weeks? Lord, who gives you so much pleasure that you just want them around?

As another example, in Psalm 19:4–6 David uses the image of the sun, comparing the sun to a bridegroom and a champion, to illustrate the power and wisdom of God:

2. A study conducted by researchers from the Edward R. Murrow School of Communication at Washington State University and the Department of Telecommunications at Indiana University concluded that "during exposure to high-imagery radio advertisements people do, in a way, see it on the radio." Paul D. Bolls and Annie Lang, "I Saw It on the Radio: The Allocation of Attention to High-Imagery Radio Advertisement," *Media Psychology* 5 (2003): 49.

> In the heavens God has pitched a tent for the sun.
>> It is like a bridegroom coming out of his chamber,
>> like a champion rejoicing to run his course.
> It rises at one end of the heavens
>> and makes its circuit to the other;
>> nothing is deprived of its warmth.

Here's how a sermon could expand these original images of bridegroom and champion:

The sun is like a bridegroom in the ancient wedding ceremony coming out of his pavilion, dressed in all his glory, on his way to his bride's house to claim her. Look at him—striding tall, dressed in splendor, accompanied by his friends and relatives, admired by the neighbors as he walks through the streets to where she and her maidens are waiting.

Or imagine a wedding today. Imagine the moment when the bride's mother has been seated, the organist strikes up the processional music, the side door opens, and the men enter and line up at the front of the room. But let's suppose that instead of the minister leading the way in a black robe, followed by the groom in a black tux, and the rest of the attendants in black tuxes, the groom leads the way in, and he's wearing a gold tux. Gold jacket, white shirt, gold bow tie, gold pants, gold shoes—he's glorious! What a specimen of manhood—a young man in all of his power and strength! That's the brilliant sun, proclaiming the glory of God.

Or maybe visualize a champion who can't wait to run his race—full of energy, muscles rippling, shaking arms and legs to loosen muscles and sinews, impatient to have the strength flow through him, lining up in the blocks, tensing for the starter's gun. Or the basketball player coming in for a dunk—look at the long steps, the soaring leap, the powerful slam of the ball through the net, the defiant walk afterward. That's the triumphant power of God!

A third example can be found in Psalm 30, where the matching chiastic units of verses 4–5 and 11–12 speak of God's turning our nighttime weeping into daylight dancing.

> Sing the praises of the LORD, you his faithful people;
>> praise his holy name.
> For his anger lasts only a moment,
>> but his favor lasts a lifetime;
> weeping may stay for the night,
>> but rejoicing comes in the morning.
> . . . . . . . . . . . . . . . . . . . . . . . . . . . . .

> You turned my wailing into dancing;
>   you removed my sackcloth and clothed me with joy,
> that my heart may sing your praises and not be silent.
>   LORD my God, I will praise you forever.

There are several original images in these lines—a momentary weeping at night, an eternal rejoicing in the morning, a funeral wailing in sackcloth, and festive wedding garments. Here's how the sermon might paint these images for the listeners:

> Weeping may come like an unwelcome guest who stays overnight. Will he never leave? Weeping may remain for a night—but it's gone in the morning, and rejoicing takes its place and stays forever.
>   "God, you turned my wailing into dancing. You took my funeral dirge, my wailing against a death I could not stop, and you turned it into a dance where we hold our arms and step in a circle to joyful music and song."
>   "You removed my sackcloth and clothed me with joy. You took off my sackcloth—that coarse, hairy, burlap shirt that was my discomfort and sorrow, and you clothed me with joy. You took off my funeral clothes, my black funeral clothes, and you dressed me in a party outfit—bright colors, high-heeled shoes, Nordstrom styles."

By thus picturesquely expanding the author's original images, we keep our listeners attentive.

## Create Contemporary Images Similar to the Author's

Sometimes, instead of expanding on the author's original image, a preacher's image may suggest a contemporary equivalent, bringing the ancient image into the present century.

For example, as we saw above in Psalm 15, David's initial question—"LORD, who may dwell in your sacred tent? Who may live on your holy mountain?"—is the equivalent of asking, "God, who would you welcome into your home? Who would you be glad to see? Who would you be so delighted to have around that you'd ask them to stay longer, maybe spend the night, or even stay for a few weeks? God, who gives you so much pleasure that you just want them around?"

In addition to expanding on the author's original images of a tent and the duration of a guest's visit, the sermon's introduction attempts to create a contemporary picture of a joyful welcome:

Whenever our grandchildren come over—when the car pulls up in the driveway or on the street curb, and the grandchildren get out of the car and come up the walkway—Nell and I open the door, clap our hands, and say, "Look who's here! Look who's here! Come in! Come in! We're so glad you came over! How are you? It's so good to see you!" And the children just know how much they are loved.

I wonder what would make God feel that way toward me? That if I started to walk into his presence, he would be standing there saying, "Oh Don, it's so good to see you! How are you? Come in! Come in! I'm so glad you came!" What would make God feel that way toward me?

What would make him feel that way toward you? What would give God so much pleasure in you that he would be anxious to have you in his presence? That he would be delighted to have you near him? What would make God feel that way toward you?

David once pondered that question. And God gave him the answer.

Luke 7:31–34 provides another example of creating a contemporary picture to convey an original image—a day at the outdoor market. In the passage, Jesus accuses the religious leaders of rejecting both him and John, despite the fact that two of them came with very different messages and lifestyles:

> Jesus went on to say, "To what, then, can I compare the people of this genera-tion? What are they like? They are like children sitting in the marketplace and calling out to each other:
>
>> "'We played the pipe for you
>>     and you did not dance;
>>  we sang a dirge,
>>     and you did not cry.'
>
> For John the Baptist came neither eating bread nor drinking wine, and you say, 'He has a demon.' The Son of Man came eating and drinking, and you say, 'Here is a glutton and a drunkard, a friend of tax collectors and sinners.'"

To make the imagery of the marketplace children come alive for today's audience, the preacher might create the following scene:

> You're like children sitting in a marketplace while their parents sell vegetables or eggs or meats. Another child comes into the market with his mother, who is going to shop for food. This child is anxious and worried. He has a baby sister that they left at home because she's sick, really sick, and isn't getting better. His parents haven't called the doctor because they don't have money. In fact, today in the market, his mother is going to shop only for the bare necessities, because that's all they can afford. His father was laid off when the landowner

he worked for sold his land to the Romans for a military training ground. The child doesn't feel like playing games or partying. But the other children in the market see him and start playing a wedding song on the flute, a dancing song, and they call out to him, "Come on, let's play weddings. Dance!" The child shakes his head. He doesn't feel like dancing. "Come on, dance!" the other children chide. He shakes his head again. Now they're upset with him. "What's the matter with him? Why doesn't he lighten up? We played the flute for him, but he won't dance." And they don't like the way he acted toward them.

That's how you were toward John, Jesus says. "Why doesn't he lighten up?" You didn't like his behavior or his sobering message.

But a little later another child comes to the marketplace. This child is on a holiday. His family's farm has produced bumper crops. His father told him he could pick out some special treats while they shopped, and for lunch they would go to an all-you-can-eat pizza buffet. And on the way home they'll buy the pet pony he's always wanted. The child comes into the market just bursting with glee at the joy of life. But now the children in the market have grown surly and cross. They've gotten themselves out of sorts. And when they see this second child, they start singing a funeral dirge. And they call to the child, "Come on, let's play funerals. We'll sing the dirge, and you beat your chest and wail and cry like a mourner." But this second child doesn't feel like crying; he's full of joy. And they're upset with him. "What's the matter with him? We sang a dirge and he didn't cry. What makes him so happy?" And they don't like the way he acted toward them.

That's how you are toward me, Jesus says. You don't like my behavior or my joyful message.

As we thus picture the author's original images in contemporary contexts, we sustain the listeners' attention.

## Visualize Contemporary Situations (Applications, Examples, Scenarios)

Listeners remain rapt whenever the speaker starts talking about what this *looks like* in our lives, how it *shows up* in our everyday circumstances, and where we would *see* it in our actual experiences. As the speaker visualizes concrete, specific, detailed, real-life scenarios, the biblical truth becomes vivid, memorable, and life-changing.[3]

For example, once again in Psalm 15, the question is "LORD, who may dwell in your sacred tent?" Part of the psalm's answer to this question is

3. Donald R. Sunukjian, *Invitation to Biblical Preaching: Proclaiming Truth with Clarity and Relevance* (Grand Rapids: Kregel, 2007), 106–27. These scenarios or pictures should not be from areas *outside* the experiences of the listeners (e.g., "illustrations" from nature, history, other cultures, etc.) but rather "applications" that surface *actual experiences* your listeners are likely to have.

> [the one] who keeps an oath even when it hurts,
>     and does not change their mind;
> who lends money to the poor without interest;
>     who does not accept a bribe against the innocent. (vv. 4–5)

Each of these lines—oaths, lending, and bribery—concern the ethical use of money. The following real-life scenarios keep the listeners' attention fixed as the truth is "applied" to contemporary experience:

> God welcomes you into his presence when you are blameless in the area of money, when all of your financial dealings show a commitment to integrity, compassion, and justice.
>
> These three specifics are spelled out in the middle of verse 4 and into verse 5. God welcomes the one "who keeps an oath even when it hurts"—that's integrity; "who lends money to the poor without interest"—that's compassion; and "who does not accept a bribe against the innocent"—that's justice.
>
> What do these mean—to keep your oath, to lend without interest, and to not accept bribes?
>
> First, to keep your oath. What pleases God is when he sees you take an oath, you give your word, and then you keep it even if it turns out to hurt you financially. You make a promise, and then stick with it, even if you lose money on the deal. To be blameless in money—committed to integrity:

> You bid on a job—building a backyard deck for someone—figuring your cost of materials and labor, and adding in a reasonable profit. You get the contract. But two days into the project, you discover you forgot to figure in the cost of varnish, and you also underestimated the hours of labor that you'll have to pay. And on the third day an unexpected rain undermines the preliminary work you've done, and you have to start all over. And suddenly you realize if you continue the project, you'll lose money on it. The price you and the homeowner agreed on won't cover the varnish, the extra labor, and the three days of wiped out work. If you walk off the job, leaving the homeowner with the forms in the ground, and raw lumber and nails lying around, you'll break even. But if you finish the job, you'll be in the hole several thousand dollars.

> You get a part-time job after school tutoring an eighth grader in math for two hours every Tuesday and Thursday afternoon, at $10 per hour; that's $40 a week. The kid is doing pretty well, pulling up his grade a bit, but the family is still worried about the final exam in two weeks. But they figure they've got two more weeks, eight more hours of help from you, and the kid should do OK. But another family suddenly discovers that their kid needs help in science, real bad and real quick, and Tuesday/Thursday afternoons are the only times they've got open. They offer you $25 an hour to come

for the next two weeks, to tutor their kid for two hours on Tuesday and Thursday afternoons. That's eight hours at $25 per hour, or $200 for the next two weeks, versus the $80 you'd make with the first family.

You agree to produce and sell 2,000 units of a product to a customer at $100 a unit—a total of $20,000. Halfway through production, another desperate customer offers you $150 a unit for what you're producing—$30,000 for the lot, $10,000 more than the price you agreed on with the original customer. The original customer is counting on them; the second customer offers you more for them. It hurts to lose the $10,000, but you gave your word.

What pleases God is when you are blameless—when you give your word and then keep it, even if it hurts you financially. You make a promise, you take an oath, and then you stick with it even if you lose money on the deal.

Blameless in money—committed to integrity, you keep your word.

And then blameless in money in another way: committed to compassion. You use your money to help, not to take advantage of others; to bless, not to burden. The beginning of verse 5: Who does God welcome? The one "who lends money to the poor without interest." Compassionate, giving someone a no-interest loan.

Now your first thought is, "All right! Find me a Christian banker who follows this. I want to meet him." Or, "Hey, this is the kind of home loan I want—principal only." Obviously we need a little explanation here.

The verse here is not talking about a business transaction. It's not talking about a commercial investment. It's not talking about a situation where both parties are financially secure.

It's talking about a needy person, a person who has been hit with financial hardship, a fellow believer who is in distress, who has a debt they must pay off or else they will have to sell themselves into slavery to provide for their family. Giving them a loan but then also charging them interest for the loan would increase their burden. It would put them further into debt; it would aggravate their distress rather than ease it. Their desperate need to pay off one creditor and get a new loan puts them at your mercy—they'll pay whatever high interest rate you charge, simply to buy a little time. Charging them interest would be taking advantage of them. You would be exploiting them or squeezing them when they had no choice.

It's like unscrupulous operators going into a disaster area—maybe North Carolina, hit by a hurricane, houses flattened, trees down, all power out for weeks. Someone from New Jersey, say, drives down with a truck full of generators that cost $200 each, but they sell them for $900 each, simply because the people are desperate to have electricity. That's what the verse is talking about here—taking advantage of someone's desperate need.

What pleases God is when he sees you are blameless and compassionate—loaning money because you want to help someone, not because you can take advantage of their predicament. Loaning freely, as an act of mercy and not as an investment opportunity. For compassion, not for gain.

Blameless in money—committed to integrity, you keep your word. Committed to compassion, you use your money to help. And third, committed to justice, you take no bribes. Recall the middle of verse 5: Who does God welcome? The one "who does not accept a bribe against the innocent."

What pleases God is when he sees that someone will not let money affect their commitment to justice—a courtroom witness who cannot be bribed to lie against the innocent, a political candidate who will not be turned against the common good by the contributions of special interest groups, a purchasing agent who won't accept kickbacks, a company worker who will not let financial considerations affect their truthfulness.

> A woman manager at your company is suing the company vice president for sexual harassment. Her lawyers are going to depose other workers in the office to see what they know about the situation. You work in her department. Your appointment with the lawyers is for this Wednesday afternoon. They're going to ask if you've witnessed any harassment by the vice president toward her. You know you have. You know she has a legitimate case. You know what your answers should be when Wednesday afternoon comes. But Tuesday morning the vice president stops by your office. He doesn't come right out and say it, but it's pretty clear—the right answers at the deposition just might get you a promotion into a managerial position, and that would mean a raise of $30,000 a year in salary.

What pleases God is when he sees you cannot be bribed against the innocent. Who does God welcome? God welcomes those who are blameless in money.

> Committed to integrity—keeping their word even if it costs them.
> Committed to compassion—using their money to help rather than take advantage.
> Committed to justice—not accepting bribes against the innocent.

In a sermon on Psalm 77, an introduction could convey contemporary experiences, matching those of the psalmist yet resonating with today's listeners. The psalmist's opening words are:

> I cried out to God for help;
>     I cried out to God to hear me.
> When I was in distress, I sought the Lord;
>     at night I stretched out untiring hands,
>     and I would not be comforted.

> I remembered you, God, and I groaned;
>     I meditated, and my spirit grew faint.
> You kept my eyes from closing;
>     I was too troubled to speak.
> I thought about the former days,
>     the years of long ago;
> I remembered my songs in the night.
>     My heart meditated and my spirit asked:
>
> "Will the Lord reject forever?
>     Will he never show his favor again?
> Has his unfailing love vanished forever?
>     Has his promise failed for all time?
> Has God forgotten to be merciful?
>     Has he in anger withheld his compassion?" (vv. 1–9)

The sermon's introduction evokes the psalmist's same thoughts, but with contemporary examples:

God seems to deal with his children in a great variety of ways. Some of us, in our physical bodies, seem to enjoy almost perfect health for most of our lives, while others are called on to endure years of pain and weakness. Similarly, in our spirits, some of us seem to enjoy almost uninterrupted peace of mind, a happiness and contentment in life, while others are made to pass through deep waters, to face an agony of spirit that is almost beyond bearing.

This morning I want to speak to this latter group—those of you whose lives are troubled, whose hearts are heavy, and who feel battered and exhausted in spirit. I want to speak to those of you who have a desperate need to know the power and love of God.

You may be going through something the rest of us can scarcely imagine. Outwardly, you are calm, but inwardly there is turmoil and fear.

It may be a marriage that is growing cold, where there is blame and bitterness. You live in the same house, but you pass each other in angry silence, as though in separate worlds.

It may be a child who seems unreachable—a child who is stubborn, defiant, determined to spurn everything that is right and pure. And any words of yours that might reach out and correct are openly and angrily cast off.

It may be your business that has come to a crisis, and you cannot break out of it. Nothing will yield to your efforts, the walls are closing in, and all you have worked for is about to be lost.

It may be a disappointment you are living with, a disappointment so large, so central to your life, something you counted on, something you dreamed of, but now seems ashes, gone forever, a disappointment that has numbed all energy and joy in life.

It may be a sin you committed, some defiling experience you stumbled into, and there is a shame that you cannot seem to erase, that keeps coming to mind.

Whatever the cause, there is some heaviness in life, and your mind churns and churns and churns with the problem, and there is no relief or rest or happiness.

Your nights are probably the worst times. You lay in bed, but sleep doesn't come. You toss and turn, you try to relax, but your mind dwells on the problem. Tears wet your eyes, and you find yourself crying with an inward pain.

You think back to happier times, when days were good and life was full of promise:

- when the marriage was sweet and sparkled with love.
- when the child was small, and laughed and clung to you and put their arms around your neck.
- when the business prospect seemed bright and without limit, when success came easily.
- when disappointment was unknown, and all was hope and plans and anticipation.

At night you lay on your bed, and from the years gone by there come memories of happier days, and you say, "God, why can't it be like that now? What happened? Why can't it be like that again?"

You have prayed to God. You've prayed long, over and over. But that has accomplished nothing. There's been no response.

You've asked for help, desperately, urgently, again and again, but there's been no answer, and nothing has changed.

And this bothers you.

Why won't God do something?
I don't understand why God lets this happen.
Why doesn't he answer me?
Where is he?
What is he doing?
Why does he let this go on like this?
Why doesn't he do something?

You are almost beside yourself with the heaviness of your burden and no help from God.

This morning I want us to look at a psalm written by a man who went through a similar experience of deep agony. He was so troubled he could not sleep. He cried at the memory of happier days. He prayed to God, desperately, but found no help, and it drove him to the point of despair.

And yet, somehow, God led him to the answer he needed, and he returned to a place of rest and trust. God led him to peace and hope, and that's what God wants to do for you.

Please turn to Psalm 77.

Here is one final example, this time from 1 Peter 3:13–15, of how creating contemporary scenarios sustains interest.

Peter begins (v. 13) by noting that godly living doesn't usually result in persecution: "Who is going to harm you if you are eager to do good?" Most of the time, if we're living like a Christian should, people generally like us and are drawn to us. The sermon could visually describe how we normally get along with people and remain free of persecution:

"At work, they tend to think highly of me. I'm a hard worker, my skills are good. I'm usually in a good mood. I work well with others. I'm willing to help them with their projects or jobs. As a result, the people at work like me. And they value me—I get good reviews and regular raises. I think I live in a godly way at work, but there's no persecution."

A student at school has the same response. "Most people at school know I'm a Christian, and they seem to respect that. They don't tease me or put me down because of it. I don't feel like I have any problem being accepted. I've played on sports teams, served in student government, been active in some of the school clubs. If I'm absent a day, I don't have trouble finding someone in class to share their notes with me. I have friends to eat with or to go to the mall with. I think I'm living a consistent Christian life at school, but I don't feel I'm being persecuted for it."

Or a young mom says, "I like my neighbors, and I think they like me. We trade babysitting. They're quick to include my kids on trips to the pool or the park. When one of us bakes something special, she sometimes makes enough to share with the rest of us. I'm active in the PTA—served on a couple of committees, organized a fundraiser for the library, cooked food for the annual carnival. I know a lot of the women, and we get along great. I think I'm acting in a godly way, and nobody's persecuting me."

However, Peter goes on to note (v. 14) that there nevertheless will be those inevitable times when our godliness will conflict with someone else's agenda, when our righteousness will stand in their way. The preacher can turn this abstract concept into pictures by visualizing some real-life scenarios, choosing some of the following from the same areas of life as those above:

At work, it may be that you and a coworker are in Las Vegas on company business. And you finish the company business in three days instead of the four days the company expected it would take. And your coworker says, "Hey, we've got a free day in Vegas. The company's not expecting us back; as far as they're concerned, we're still working. What do you say we stay the extra day to take in a show or hit the blackjack tables? Have some fun? You know, 'What happens in Vegas stays in Vegas.'" And you say, "Nah, if you want, you can stay, but I'm going to head back." And he says, "What do you mean I can stay if I want! If you want to go back, I have to go back. Man, what a wet blanket you are." And from then on, he's hostile to you at work—uncooperative, frequently putting you down in front of others, paying you back for your "goody-goody" attitude that spoiled his fun. If you live in a godly manner, at some point it will conflict with someone else's sin, and you will be persecuted.

Maybe someone in the office comes around collecting for a housewarming gift for the secretary who just moved in with her boyfriend. If you pass on that, could it create ill will in the office?

At school, it may be a student who grabs you just before you go into class and says, "Hey, I didn't have a chance to do the homework of looking up resources in the library and writing down the call numbers of the books. Sit with me in the back of the room. Let me copy your page real fast before we have to turn them in." And you say, "Aaahhh, I don't think I'd feel good about doing that." And he says, "Hey man, I let you copy my notes when you were absent; let me copy your answers." And you say, "It's not the same thing. I wouldn't mind letting you copy my class notes, but a homework assignment is kinda different." He says, "Forget it," and he stomps into class. And from then on, whenever you make a comment in class that reflects your Christian beliefs, he's got some snide, ridiculing statement to make that gets a laugh out of the rest of the class.

Maybe the substitute teacher is being given the runaround by the class. The class is telling her that the assignment is not due today, but you're sitting there and you know that it *is* due today and that the regular teacher said the substitute would collect it. Should you say something and risk the wrath of the class?

Or maybe one night while you're at a PTA meeting, the topic comes up of including alternative lifestyle literature in the sixth-grade reading program—books with titles like *Johnny Has Two Daddies* or *Both My Mommies Love Me*. And you think to yourself, "I don't really think I want my sixth-grade daughter reading that." And so you raise your hand and stand and, as gracefully as you can, try to say something like, "I wonder if some parents, in good conscience, would rather handle these issues at home and not have their children influenced at school toward some of these views. I wonder if we could leave it up to each home to decide what they want to communicate to their children regarding these issues." And then, before you sit down, there's an undercurrent of negative comments—with the words "homophobic" and "intolerant" and some scattered hissing or booing. And from then on at PTA meetings, nobody wants to get too close to you or seem to be too much of a friend, lest others heap the same scorn on them.

Maybe your daughter is invited to a birthday party for her friend down the block, and you find out that the girl's mother is planning to show a PG-13 video that has scenes you'd prefer your children not see. "Should I keep my daughter at home and maybe antagonize a neighbor?"

If you live in a godly way, at some point it will conflict with someone else's sin, and you will be persecuted.

In such situations, Peter's first encouragement (vv. 14–15) is, "'Do not fear their threats; do not be frightened.' But in your hearts revere Christ as Lord." Don't fear what other people would normally fear in such situations: the unpleasant consequences, the possible threat, the potential loss of esteem or friendship or even a job.

Again, by asking yourself "What would this *look like*? How would this fear *show up* in my listeners' experiences?" you might come up with something like the following:

Somebody at work starts telling a joke. We figure out pretty quickly that it's probably going to be a dirty joke. And we want to say to him that we'd rather not hear it, but we know if we do, he'll give us a disgusted look, go to the next guy, and say, "Hey, you want to hear a good joke?" And then, after he tells it, he'll say, "Isn't that good? Joe over there has 'virgin ears' and didn't want to hear it." We have a tendency to fear what most people would fear in that situation—the disdain and ridicule. And we'd be tempted to let that fear control what we do.

Or one of our nieces or nephews is marrying an unbeliever, and they ask if they can have the wedding reception in our backyard. We know that if we say no on biblical grounds—believers are to marry only other believers—it'll cause a stink not only with them but also with all the rest of the family and relatives. We have a tendency to fear what most people would fear in that situation—the anger and unpleasantness. And we'd be tempted to let that fear control what we do.

Instead of fearing, Peter says, we are to determine that Christ is going to be the Lord of our life, and that he will determine how we act, not them. We're going to be more concerned about his reaction than anyone else's.

Peter's second encouragement (v. 15) is to be ready to give an explanation if someone asks why you're willing to let such grief come on you when you could just as easily avoid it by going along. "Always be prepared to give an answer to everyone who asks you to give the reason for the hope that you have. But do this with gentleness and respect."

Someone else watches you take a stand and pay a price. And they ask, "Why would you bother to do that?"
Someone in the office says, "Why not stay the extra day in Vegas so you don't have to listen to his bad mouth back at the office?"

Someone in the class says, "Why not let him copy your answers so that
he doesn't torment you the rest of the semester?"

At the PTA meeting, someone comes up to you and asks, "What difference
does it make? Let them add the books to the sixth-grade reading program. Why get yourself ostracized by half the parents at the school?"

At work, the guy at the next desk says, "Why not just drop five bucks into
the collection cup? You don't think they're the only ones moving in
together, do you? Why be called the prude of the office?"

One of your relatives asks, "Why not let them have the wedding reception
in your backyard rather than be on the outs with the whole family?"

What would a gentle and respectful answer sound like in some of the above
scenarios? Listeners will soak up any help the preacher can give as to the *actual words* that could be used. And so the preacher, continuing the concrete
pictures, offers something along the following lines:

"I knew when I came back from Vegas I was disappointing Bob, and I hated to
do that. But in terms of my own Christian faith, I felt I had to be honest with
the company."

"I knew when I said that at the PTA meeting that I would get a lot of grief.
But I just don't want to see our kids influenced toward something the Bible calls
unnatural and sinful. Down through history, whenever that kind of behavior
became prominent in a nation, God judged that nation, and it ceased to exist.
Historically it's happened several times. And I don't want that to happen to
our country."

"I know the relatives are mad at me about the wedding reception. But I can't
celebrate something the Bible says not to do. And I know there's nothing more
critical to the happiness of our kids than marrying another believer. When my
kids see how much I believe that, and that I'm willing to stand for it even if it
costs me, then they know that I won't support them either if they moved in
that direction. And knowing that will help them turn away from that sorrow
and move in God's direction. I'm willing to take the grief because I want my
kids to have the greatest possible joy in life."

## Conclusion

God gave us stories. Jesus gave us parables. Paul gave us sports metaphors.
James spoke of a rich person visiting church. Pictures! Pictures! Pictures! And
the people will hear us gladly!

# Afterword

## *The Worlds of the Preacher*

### SCOTT M. GIBSON

This volume provides the preacher with tools to explore the different worlds in which he or she lives. The various authors examined the four worlds suggested by Haddon Robinson—the ancient world of the Bible, the modern world, the world of the preacher's listeners, and the preacher's personal world.

Readers now see how Robinson's homiletical lens of the four worlds of the preacher provides a helpful introduction to the ongoing task of preaching. The contributors themselves recognize the multi-textured and challenging task it is to preach God's Word responsibly.

For now, the history, language, and culture of these worlds open up even more possibilities for further investigation. Steven Mathewson and Duane Litfin provided helpful approaches to discovering the world of the Old and New Testaments. My chapter on the character of the preacher provides ways to tend to one's inner world, all the while engaging with others in a life of discipleship. Matthew Kim raised important questions for preachers as they engage the culture—questions that need to be asked of ourselves and of our churches. The world of the listener was helpfully addressed by Jeffrey Arthurs as he applied Robinson's homiletic to the functional questions. Patricia Batten demonstrated that knowing one's present world makes an important difference in how to preach and how one is perceived as a preacher. Victor Anderson pushed preachers to recognize the immense impact of the mission of God in preaching. The significance of history in the task of preaching was named by Scott Wenig—and he is right! Finally, Donald Sunukjian masterfully imaged for us examples of preaching that keeps listeners attentive to God's truth as they live in an image-filled age.

The chapters in this book comprise a stretching, an elongation, a broadening of what Haddon Robinson first discussed in his important lecture "The Worlds of the Preacher." These four worlds will remain for the preacher, and further engagement with them will be necessary for those who preach in the future and for those who hear. This is the task of homiletics: to continue to strive to understand the mission of preaching and to make it intellectually viable, spiritually stimulating, and practically relevant in our present time and on into the future.

# Contributors

**Victor D. Anderson** (PhD, Biola University) is department chair and professor of pastoral ministries at Dallas Theological Seminary, Dallas, Texas.

**Jeffrey Arthurs** (PhD, Purdue University) is professor of preaching and communication at Gordon-Conwell Theological Seminary, South Hamilton, Massachusetts.

**Patricia M. Batten** (DMin, Gordon-Conwell Theological Seminary) is adjunct assistant professor of preaching at Gordon-Conwell Theological Seminary, South Hamilton, Massachusetts.

**Scott M. Gibson** (DPhil, University of Oxford) is the Haddon W. Robinson Professor of Preaching and Ministry and director of the Haddon W. Robinson Center for Preaching at Gordon-Conwell Theological Seminary, South Hamilton, Massachusetts.

**Matthew D. Kim** (PhD, University of Edinburgh) is associate professor of preaching and ministry at Gordon-Conwell Theological Seminary, South Hamilton, Massachusetts.

**Duane Litfin** (PhD, Purdue University; DPhil, University of Oxford) is president emeritus of Wheaton College (Illinois). He taught preaching for ten years at Dallas Theological Seminary and has pastored churches in Indiana and Tennessee.

**Steven D. Mathewson** (DMin, Gordon-Conwell Theological Seminary) is associate director of the doctor of ministry program at Western Seminary and senior pastor of CrossLife Evangelical Free Church in Libertyville, Illinois.

**Haddon W. Robinson** (1931–2017) (PhD, University of Illinois) was the Harold John Ockenga Distinguished Professor of Preaching, senior director of the doctor of ministry program, and former interim president at Gordon-Conwell Theological Seminary.

**Donald R. Sunukjian** (ThD, Dallas Theological Seminary; PhD, University of California at Los Angeles) is professor of preaching at Talbot School of Theology, Biola University, La Mirada, California.

**Scott Wenig** (PhD, University of Colorado) is the Haddon W. Robinson Chair of Biblical Preaching and professor of applied theology at Denver Seminary, Denver, Colorado.